Showing of Love

Julian of Norwich

Showing of Love

Translated from the British Library Sloane 2499 Manuscript (S)

Collated with the Westminster Cathedral Manuscript (W),
the Paris, Bibliothèque Nationale, Anglais 40 Manuscript (P),
and the British Library, Additional 37,790,
Amherst Manuscript (A)

by
Julia Bolton Holloway

A Michael Glazier Book

THE LITURGICAL PRESS
Collegeville, Minnesota

www.litpress.org

A Michael Glazier Book published by The Liturgical Press.

Cover design by Ann Blattner. Photo credits: Westminster Julian Manuscript, by permission of Westminster Cathedral; Julian of Norwich icon by Father Nathanael, courtesy http://www.umilta.net; other photos courtesy Julia Bolton Holloway.

1   2   3   4   5   6   7   8

Library of Congress Cataloging-in-Publication Data

Julian, of Norwich, b. 1343.
    [Revelations of divine love. English]
    Showing of love / Julian of Norwich ; translated from the British Library Sloane 2499 manuscript (S), collated with the Westminster Cathedral manuscript (W), the Paris, Bibliotheque nationale, Anglais 40 manuscript (P), and the British Library Amherst manuscript (A) by Julia Bolton Holloway.
        p. cm.
    "A Michael Glazier book."
    Includes bibliographical references.
    ISBN 0-8146-5169-0 (alk. paper)
    1. Devotional literature, English (Middle)   2. Love—Religious aspects—Christianity—Early works to 1800.   3. Private revelations—Early works to 1800.   4. Julian, of Norwich, b. 1343.   I. Holloway, Julia Bolton, 1937–
II. Title.

BV4831.J8213 2003
242—dc21

2003040058

To Our Lord God

Who Has in Us

His Homeliest Home

and

His Endless Dwelling

Preface

I. On Julian of Norwich

Books written by Julian of Norwich and by Margery Kempe of Lynn, who knew each other, open windows into their medieval world. It was a world that embraced East Anglia's Norwich and Lynn and, with Margery of Lynn, also Rome, Gdansk, Bergen, Cologne, Compostela, Jerusalem, and Bethlehem, indeed all Christendom and beyond—a world in which women could be writers of theology or at least recognized for their holiness, women such as Hildegard of Bingen and Marguerite Porete, Angela of Foligno and Catherine of Siena, Birgitta of Sweden and Mary of Oignies. When the two East Anglian women conversed with each other, Julian repeated to Margery that God sits in our soul as a fair city. Sigmund Freud, in *Civilization and Its Discontents,* gave as metaphor for the mind the city of Rome, as it once was, as it is now, as it will be, all palimpsested, all simultaneously layered, one upon the other, then dismissed the image as nonsense. But we shall find Julian's hermitage within her city, though a paradox, to make profound sense, her book to be of soul-healing. She makes of Norwich Nazareth, Bethlehem, Jerusalem, so palimpsesting the Bible upon England. Her city is every city, Mary its queen, Christ its king. We present her book here with its palimpsested layers, giving her text's rich and variant readings.

We learn, in the *Showing of Love* and elsewhere, of the anchorhold with its three small windows, in the graveyard of St. Julian's Church, nestled against the thatched roof of that church, the rain pouring down its eaves, and also of the herring that would have been shipped up the River Wensum, at the bottom of the street of St. Julian's Alley. For Julian compares the commonplace raindrops and herring of Norwich to the flowing out from God of Christ's redeeming blood. Today the area about her cell is bombed out, its church rebuilt. But once this was a bustling community of great learning and England's second largest city. We know she had women, named Alice and Sara, who lived with her and shopped for her, for they were left money in wills. We can imagine them borrowing books for her from the Augustinians by the river, shopping for parchment for her in Parmenter Street. To one side, on its knoll, is Norwich Castle, to the other, beside river meadows, is the Cathedral of the Holy and Undivided Trinity, whose Benedictine monks had oversight over Carrow Priory with St. Julian's Church and its anchorhold. A Cambridge University Library manuscript contains schoolboy drawings by Adam Easton of both Castle and Cathedral in Norwich and how to measure them by trigonometry. As a Norwich Benedictine, Easton next taught Hebrew at Oxford and in 1381 became Cardinal of England, with his titular church at Santa Cecilia in Trastevere. He knew John Whiterig and Thomas Brinton in England, and William Flete, Alfonso of Jaén, Birgitta of Sweden, and Catherine of Siena in Italy.

Julian's writings and their preservation reveal strong links with Benedictinism. She quotes from Gregory's *Dialogues* giving the miracle of St. Benedict in prayer, where the whole world becomes reduced to a single beam of light, it being explained that in the presence of the Creator all that is created "seems full little." Julian's writings reflect those of Adam Easton himself and likewise the books in his library, for she, too, knew Hebrew and the Victorine edition of the mystical writings of Pseudo-Dionysius, John Whiterig's *Meditationes*, William Flete's *Remedies against Sin*, the *Dialogo* of Catherine of Siena, and the *Revelationes* of Birgitta of Sweden, edited by Alfonso of Jaén. In one of Adam Easton's manuscripts, on canon law, he makes notes about a deformed, crippled woman. She writes about her great pain, both physical and mental, and of her "wanting of will" (a true definition of depression), her desire to die when young. Adam Easton and Julian of Norwich together write on the Hebrew meanings of the name "Adam" as meaning "Everyman," "Everywoman," and "clay" and "red," and on the meaning of God's name as "I am, I it am." In the *Life of Christina of Markyate* we learn that Benedictines initiated conversation with the one saying "Benedicite," the other replying "Dominus." Julian several times says this in her text, "Benedicite Dominus." The title Margery gives to her, "Dame Julian," is that of a Benedictine nun. Her manuscripts were to be secretly preserved from destruction in Brigittine and Benedictine convents in England and in exile.

A brilliant crippled woman in medieval Norwich could have been useful to Benedictine Carrow Priory, which supported itself with boarding young girls and educating them, some among them named "Julian," several of these in turn becoming their nuns. Julian's autobiographical writings speak of her "service in youth" to God, and also of considerable illnesses, these being so burdensome that she desires to die early, stressing this in all three versions of her *Showing of Love*. Her desire was partly granted, a devastating illness afflicting her on 8 or 13 May 1373 (one manuscript has "viii," the other "xiii"), when she was just past thirty, and under her family's roof. But she lives to tell its tale, twice over, at fifty, in 1393, and at seventy, in 1413. Her autobiography becomes like Tolstoy's "Death of Ivan Ilyich," like Boethius' *Consolation of Philosophy,* like Augustine's *Confessions,* like the books of Job and of Jonah. But it also swirls about medieval Norwich. In her dessicating, hallucinating fever, immediately after the "religious person" (a Benedictine monk), has visited her, she has a horrific vision of the fiend, who comes with hair like red unscored rust, his skin freckled with black spots like burnt tile stones, clutching her by the throat, while she still believes in God. A similar tale was told in Norwich, recorded in a Lambeth Palace Syon Abbey manuscript, of such a vision in 1350 to a man who had earlier seen written in a book of the need to pray to the Virgin, and who then does so when being throttled by the devil, who therefore has to release him. Julian's vision recalls another by St. Birgitta, concerning evil cardinals as like freckled, burnt tile stones and rust, Birgitta being told they may not preside at the altar while they are in sin. Pope John Paul II, for whom 13 May is also significant, specifically cited this vision by Birgitta when proclaiming her Co-Patroness of Europe.

It is likely that Julian, unable for health and social reasons to become fully a choir nun at Carrow, earned her keep by teaching, both before and after her illness, until Archbishop Chancellor Arundel's 1407–1409 Constitutions would forbid her doing so. Her writings throughout center most of all in the themes of learning and teaching, and twice she mentions theology as like an "ABC." The medieval tradition has St. Anne teach the Virgin to read, then Mary teach Jesus his letters and his prayers. Women, especially anchoresses, taught boys in Dame schools their ABC, their catechism, their Latin, from which foundation men could then enter the Church as monks and as priests, even becoming scholars, bishops, cardinals, popes. It is also possible that Julian once journeyed as a pilgrim to Rome and saw there the Veronica Veil, the Vernicle, which she describes so movingly in her vision of Christ. This relic, kept in St. Peter's and written about also by Dante and Petrarch, is now lost, the Holy Year of 2000 substituting for it the Holy Shroud of Turin. Had she visited Rome she would likely, from her Benedictine associations, have stayed with the Benedictine nuns at Santa Cecilia in Trastevere, for this was Adam Easton's titular church in Rome as cardinal and where his retinue, including many from Norwich, lodged, conveniently across the Tiber (Tras-tevere), close to the Vatican.

The "religious person" who laughed at her bedside, then became serious about her vision in 1373, and who is mentioned in the Paris, Sloane, and Amherst Manuscripts, could have been Adam Easton. He could also have been "the man of holy Church" who told her of St. Cecilia and of the martyr's three wounds with a sword, mentioned in the 1413 Amherst Manuscript. Adam Easton was likely in England at the date of Julian's vision in May 1373, and were she his sister and thought to be dying, having been sent away, a failure, from Carrow Priory, he could have visited her under their mother's roof. His brilliant career at Oxford, interrupted with several years of preaching very effectively in Norwich against the mendicant Franciscan, Dominican, Augustinian, and Carmelite Friars, had next taken him to the papal Curia in Avignon and Rome. He had been made cardinal in 1381 in exchange for his finely written book on the power of the Pope, *Defensorium ecclesiastice potestatis*, in which he displays his Hebrew and Pseudo-Dionysian learning. In 1382 he arranged the Coronation of King Richard II and Queen Anne of Bohemia, daughter of the Emperor Charles, in Westminster Abbey, for which he helped write the *Liber Regalis*, which is still used in British coronations. It was a brilliant record, save for his rather underhanded plotting against John Wyclif with the Pope. Meanwhile, Pope Urban VI was struggling to reform the cardinals, who rebelled against him.

Then the Pope, in 1385, in a rage, threw six cardinals into a dungeon and had them tortured. One of these was Adam Easton. The English Benedictine congregation, Parliament, Oxford University, and King Richard II all wrote impassioned letters pleading that Adam's life be spared and his benefices restored, comparing him to the wounded traveler in the parable of the Good Samaritan, and begging that the Pope bind up his wounds with wine and oil. The other five cardinals all met their deaths, Easton being the only one left alive. He remained a prisoner from 1385 until Boniface IX restored him in 1389, at which point he returned home to Norwich to carry out his vow made in his dungeon to St. Birgitta (who had died 21 July 1373 in Rome on her return from Jerusalem), that he would work for her canonization if she would spare his life. I believe Cardinal Adam Easton then edited Julian's Long Text, preserved in the Sloane Manuscripts, inscribing its table of contents, its admiring chapter divisions, and its colophon, having been in Norwich with Birgitta's *Revelationes* and other books shipped from the Lowlands during the writing of the Long Text *Showing of Love,* while he himself was composing the canonization document validating Birgitta of Sweden's writing of similar visions to Europe. He then died in Rome and is buried in Santa Cecilia in Trastevere. At his death in 1397 Julian would have lost her powerful patron.

Adam Easton and John Wyclif, both of Oxford University, had become deeply opposed to each other, Easton waging an intense campaign against Wyclif. Wyclif desired that the Church return to the Gospel, that it use the vernacular in the liturgy so that common men and women could understand the Bible, and that it cease from seeking wealth and power, its university-trained priests instead living learned, simple lives amidst their parishes, caring for and educating their flock. (The Second Vatican Council, centuries later, followed through on many of Wyclif's proposed reforms.) Easton, on the other hand, from his readings of Pseudo-Dionysius and from his Benedictine heritage supported the hierarchy of the Pope and the Church and the right of Benedictine monasteries to own rich possessions. He instigated the persecution of the Wycliffites, also known as "Lollards," having earlier preached against the mendicant Orders present in Norwich. A few bishops became rabidly anti-Wycliffite, including Bishop Le Despenser of Norwich and Bishop Thomas Brinton, O.S.B., of Rochester, Easton's fellow monk at Norwich and fellow student at Oxford, and, following these men, the powerful Archbishop of Canterbury and Chancellor of England, Thomas Arundel, who in 1407–1409 cracked down on Wycliffite Lollards, for political reasons, as both heretics and traitors, forbidding unlicensed lay people the Bible or the liturgy or theological writings in English, insisting on pilgrimages to relics and on prayers only in uncomprehended Latin instead of in English, the laity's "mother tongue," and being particularly draconian against learning in women. Already the first Lollard to be burnt in chains at the stake at Smithfield, as both heretic and traitor, in 1401, was Thomas Sawtre, Margery Kempe's curate at St. Margaret's in Lynn, who had been hounded by both Le Despenser of Norwich and Arundel of Canterbury. Thomas Sawtre was convicted for believing he should worship the incarnate Christ rather than a painted wooden crucifix. At the Reformation it would be the Catholics' turn to be so rabidly persecuted. Books, among them Julian's *Showing,* were destroyed, along with bodies, in the process.

It was during Arundel's persecution of the unlicensed laity that Julian would have lost her income derived from teaching young boys their ABC, their Latin, their catechism, their Bible, and that loss of support is reflected in the flurry of wills in 1394, 1404, 1415, and 1416, leaving money for her survival as anchoress of St. Julian's Church in Norwich. The final will leaving funds for Julian was written by the Countess of Suffolk, Isabella Ufford, and had as its executor Sir Miles Stapleton, whose daughter, Lady Emma Stapleton, in turn became the anchoress to the Carmelites in Norwich and for whom it is possible that the Amherst Manuscript was first assembled. Julian would also have had to dramatically revise her life work, the *Showing of Love*. Every page had translated passages from the Bible into English, and this was now strictly forbidden upon pain of burning at the stake as a Lollard. The final, Amherst, version notes that painted wooden crucifixes are to be worshiped, speaks emphatically of the **Pater Noster, Ave,** and **Credo,** and removes from itself swathes and swathes of translations into English from the Bible. The great sadness is that Adam Easton had translated the Bible from Hebrew into Latin, correcting Jerome's errors; then his Bible was stolen from him. He had criticized Wyclif for being unscholarly and for translating Jerome's Latin errors into English rather than going directly to the Hebrew. Julian too is translating from the Hebrew, not into Latin but into English, centuries before the King James Bible. Her *Showing's* "All shall be well," said to her by Christ, translates the Hebrew *shalom.* The Vulgate and the Wyclif Bibles give this merely as *recte* and "right." Julian and the Anglican King James Bible's translators got it right.

Perhaps we do not know her real name, for she may have taken the name of the male saint of St. Julian's Church. There is a manuscript speaking of the similar visions of one Mary Westwick, spelling this name "Oestwyck," while Adam Easton spelled his "Oeston." The Westwick area near the castle had been Norwich's Jewry from 1144–1290, before their expulsion by King John. This Jewry had funded the building of Norwich Cathedral. A remnant, perhaps as converts married into Christian Norwich families, could have survived, and Julian may have stemmed from one of these families. Julian and Adam may have shared the Jewish heritage of the Carmelites Teresa of Avila and Edith Stein.

II. On Her *Showing of Love*

The manuscripts of the *Showing of Love* have internal indications as to the dates when she wrote their original versions. The Westminster Cathedral Manuscript (𝕎), copied out later but having the date "1368" on the first folio, could indeed have originally been written then, before the 1373 vision, since it presents her theology, speaking of her desire to die young and God agreeing. She would then have been 25. Other contemplative women have been similarly precocious. One thinks of Catherine of Siena and Thérèse of Lisieux. It contains in its abbreviated form Julian's essential theology, Mary contemplating her yet unborn child with the "O Sapientia" Advent antiphon, the hazelnut in the palm of her hand, Jesus as our Mother, her desire to die young, her wanting a vision of the crucifix. That same 1368 is the year of Birgitta's vision of the crucifix that spoke to her in the Lateran. The Westminster Manuscript significantly lacks the deathbed visions and the Parable Showing of the Lord and the Servant.

The Sloane (S) and Paris (P) Manuscripts contain the Long Text of Julian of Norwich's *Showing of Love*. Within this form of the text she explains that her deathbed vision took place in May of 1373, and that she then contemplated upon it for from fifteen (S) (1388) to twenty years (P) (1393), performing this book of her *Showing of Love*, finishing its final version when she was fifty. These manuscripts contain all of the Westminster version of her text, boilerplating onto its theology the series of visions as narrative frame that she had when she and those with her thought she was dying. She was inclined to doubt the validity of these visions, but mentioned to "a religious person" that she had seen the crucifix "bleed fast." He, who had been laughing, immediately took her seriously, about which she was in anguish.

Julian thus begins writing the Long Text while Adam Easton is still a prisoner of his Pope. She completes it when Cardinal Adam Easton is finally able to return to Norwich, bringing books with him, and where he settles down to write his Defense of Birgitta of Sweden, *Defensorium Sanctae Birgittae*, 1389–1391. Birgitta had spent a lifetime, from the age of forty to the age of seventy, writing a massive tome in many books about her visions, some of which she had had as a child in Sweden; she had traveled to Italy, lived in Rome, then pilgrimaged to Jerusalem and Bethlehem in the last year of her life. Her *Revelationes* had first been brought to England and likely to Norwich in 1348, where Adam Easton as a young monk of eighteen could have first seen them, when she sought to end the Hundred Years War between the kings of France and England. Adam Easton now returned to Norwich in 1389 with a fine copy of Birgitta of Sweden's *Revelationes* from which he culled the argument for her canonization, collating this with that already written by Bishop Hermit Alfonso of Jaén, which is filled with cross-references like those in Julian's Long Text *Showing*, and with chapter headings similar to those in the Sloane Manuscripts.

These chapter headings in the *Showing of Love* are not written by Julian, but by her editor who admires her. He may well be Adam Easton, who is attempting to have her write a book similar to that of Birgitta of Sweden. There are direct echoes of the *Revelationes* in the *Showing*, but more of these are to be found in the Sloane chapter headings than in the Sloane and Paris text. Moreover, Julian constructs the Parable of the Lord and the Servant in such a way that it evokes the coronation pageantry of the *Liber Regalis* and the punishing of Adam Easton with imprisonment and torture by his Pope. Adam Easton's own *Defensorium Ecclesiastice Potestatis* had emphasized the mirroring between earth and heaven, between kings, emperors, bishops, popes, and God. Julian seems cognizant of all these works and likewise of the letters sent pleading for the life of Adam Easton and the restoration of his benefices, citing the parable of the Good Samaritan. Nor was the treatment of Adam Easton the only atrocity of which Julian would have known. She likely witnessed the drawing of malefactors along the cobbled flint streets of Norwich before their being hung and quartered. She describes in her hallucinatory crucifix vision the effects of such drawing and hanging as palimpsested upon the face and body of Christ. John Litester, the "King of the Commons" during the Peasants' Revolt, was so executed by Julian's Bishop of Norwich, Le Despenser, who commemorated it with a gift to the cathedral of the Despenser Retable, showing Christ's crucifixion. (John Gay's *Beggar's Opera* makes a similar analogy between Tyburn's executions and Christ's.) Religiously and politically, public bodily mutilation was used to terrorize people into obedience, in Christ's day to the Roman empire, in Julian's day to prevent rebellion against state and church. In part Julian's text is therapy for trauma abuse syndrome. Like Viktor Frankl, Holocaust survivor, she is a doctor for troubled souls. She, having healed her own soul through writing her own book, the *Showing of Love*, can and does heal those of others.

By 1413 Julian's situation had changed. Cardinal Adam Easton had died in 1397. Archbishop Chancellor Arundel, for political more than for religious reasons, was forbidding upon pain of death so much of what was contained in the earlier *Showing of Love*, the Bible and theology in the vernacular, teaching by a woman, the concentrating on the crucified Christ rather than upon wooden painted crosses. *Piers Plowman* had to be revised during this period in a censored and shorter version to survive at all. Julian at seventy, with the help of a Carmelite scribe, similarly revises her *Showing of Love* and it appears in abbreviated form in a manuscript forming a gathering of contemplative texts perhaps for such a person as Lady Emma Stapleton. The Amherst Manuscript (Ⱨ) also contains Marguerite Porete's *Mirror of Simple Souls,* Jan Van Ruusbroec's *Sparkling Stone,* as well as fragments from Henry Suso's *Horologium Sapientiae* and from Birgitta of Sweden's *Revelationes,* all of these writers associated with the "Friends of God" circle, as if this manuscript were representing Julian's own contemplative library. This Amherst Short Text version lacks "Jesus as Mother," the Parable of the Lord and the Servant, and much of the material translating the Bible. Yet it crystallizes Julian's mature thought and exemplifies her courage, for by using the Lollard term "even-Christians" Julian courted burning by Arundel. She ends this text so, bravely adding "Amen," knowing its Hebrew meaning as affirming what is said, what is spoken, what is done, what is created. We, as the royal priesthood, as the one body of Christ, say and live this word become flesh when we receive the Host.

III. On Her Contemplative Theology

Julian as a laywoman could only have received that Host fifteen times a year, but would daily, as an anchoress, have witnessed and worshiped it through her window looking onto the altar at St. Julian's Church. She shapes her text upon the Word as far as a woman can, remembering that Mary was present at the birth and at the death of Jesus, and that she thought upon all these things in her heart, having "mind" of his death and his birth. Daily Julian would have contemplated the Bible, its Hebrew Scriptures, its Psalms, and in Latin its Gospel, Acts, and Epistles. Texts associated with her, the Norwich Castle Manuscript, the *Showing of Love* manuscripts, the *Book of Margery Kempe,* show her as catechist and prophet (both allowed to women in the New Testament), and as spiritual director (to a woman). In *lectio divina* with her book she mirrors herself and ourselves into "compassion" with the Incarnation and the Passion, into the "imitation of Christ" sought through the body, mind, and soul of his Mother—and our own.

George Eliot wrote in *Middlemarch:*

"How will you know the pitch of that great bell
Too large for you to stir? Let but a flute
Play 'neath the fine-mixed metal: listen close

Till the right note flows forth, a silvery rill:
Then shall the huge bell tremble—then the mass
With myriad waves concurrent shall respond
In low soft unison."

Julian's visionary Parable of the Lord and the Servant is the parable of the entire Bible, from Adam to Christ, and of the Incarnation and Resurrection. Her text centers on the Incarnation, beginning with the Annunciation to Mary, her pregnancy with Christ, her contemplation, in *lectio divina,* of her coming child, as mirroring Julian's conception and birth of her book of the *Showing of Love.* That image she takes from Marguerite Porete's *Mirror of Simple Souls.* Many current studies of Julian of Norwich dive deep into obscure waters of "soteriology." Julian, instead, knew how to use simple words to present profound concepts clearly, to be like George Eliot's silver flute in harmony with the great bell. She knew her Bible, including its Isaiah on the Suffering Servant, inside out and sideways. Julian of Norwich and Birgitta of Sweden both had access to scholars of Hebrew; likewise Elizabeth Barrett Browning and George Eliot brought their brilliance to women's books, casting them in the mold of theology, writing them for all. Julian, as we have said, probably taught small children their alphabet and their catechism. A manuscript survives in Norwich Castle that is not the *Showing of Love,* but a translation into Middle English of the letter Jerome (actually Pelagius) wrote to "The Maid Demetriade who had vowed virginity" and catechetical works that may have been written by her, for its hand matches the corrections to the Amherst 1413 Manuscript. This Norwich Castle Manuscript has capitals in gold on a purple ground. It includes a discussion of the Hebrew meanings of "Amen." It deserves far more study than it has received. Julian likely also knew some of the most brilliant men in England and certainly receives the admiration of one of them who is editing her text with comments to each chapter. She is simple and she is profound. And she is the more profound for presenting this Magnificat, balancing Christ's Beatitudes, as a woman, thus sharing Mary's gender and joy and desolation and glory.

She speaks of Christ our brother and of "Master Jesus." Julian combines Adam and Christ. She then blends Mary and Christ, having Christ be our mother into whom we are all born, reflecting the Gospel of John's dialogue between Christ and Nicodemus. (Her first editor into print, Serenus Cressy, O.S.B., went even further and called her "Mother Julian.") Yet her language is pre-women's liberation, insisting that masculine forms include the feminine, as they do in Latin and other Mediterranean languages. For example:

> For in our Mother Christ we profit and increase, and in mercy he reforms and restores us, and by the virtue of his Passion and his death and Uprising, ones us to our substance. Thus works our Mother in mercy to all his children who are pliant and obedient.

She explains this by saying "Adam" means not just the single Adam, but all men and all women, as is true of its Hebrew meaning, and that where she says "we" she again means all men and women, and that Christ Jesus is Holy Mother Church. Joan of Arc, Margery Kempe's contemporary, would say the same to Norwich's bishop at her trial. In Julian's day one could only be Christian in Christendom, Jews having been banished from England on pain of death, so to describe her relation with "mankind" she speaks of our "even-Christian," that we are all one, all his brothers, his sisters, his mothers, as Christ said of us. In Christ's parable of the Good Samaritan one's "even-Christian" is all humanity.

In the Parable of the Lord and the Servant Julian sees God seated on the ground and dressed in blue. That was the iconography of the Virgin in her humility, begun at Avignon by Simone Martini for Cardinal Stefaneschi, showing the Virgin seated on the earth, in a wilderness, and dressed in blue, with the cardinal himself in his scarlet robes kneeling before her, present within the scene as donor. That iconography is echoed in the Wilton Diptych showing Richard II kneeling as donor, in a wilderness, with his patron saints, before the blue-clad Virgin and Child who are surrounded by angels. For Julian this blueness also reflects the letter (*Epistola* LXXVII) Jerome wrote to Fabiola at her request explaining to her the garb of the high priest Aaron (Exod 28:31), stressing his hyacinthine blue robes, a document Adam Easton used in his *Defensorium Ecclesiastice Potestatis.* Mary and Christ our high priest palimpsest one upon the other, in compassion with the Passion, and so do we join them, "oneing" ourselves into this mystery. Julian likewise centers on the Trinity, noting that wherever she speaks of one Person all three are signified and contained. Norwich's cathedral is dedicated to the Holy and Undivided Trinity. Adam Easton as Benedictine in the Cathedral Priory of the Holy and Undivided Trinity of Norwich would have preached often throughout Norwich on this topic.

In Julian's day the Church taught that Jews were damned unless converts. Julian bravely says she cannot see this in her vision. As we have seen, it may be that Julian's own family had roots in Norwich's Jewry. Certainly her text uses parts of the Jewish *Shema*, "Hear, O Israel, the Lord our God is one Lord, And you shall love the Lord your God with all your heart, and with all your soul, and with all your might," over and over again, going on to teach this as the *Shema* itself bids us do. Another prayer, the first a Jewish child like Jesus would be taught, is "Into your hands I commend my spirit." Mary, who taught it to him when he was a child, then heard him repeat her words as she stood beneath him while he was dying on the cross. Julian fills her text with images of God's hands, which become her own holding the hazelnut that is all God's creation. In Hebrew the letter *yod*, ׳, also means hand, and ten, and is the smallest letter of the Hebrew alphabet and begins God's name, and Julian's.

> The sweet gracious hands of our Mother be ready and diligent about us. For he in all this working uses the office of a natural nurse and has nought else to do but to attend to the salvation of her Child.

Julian's *Showing of Love* shows awareness of the original Hebrew of the Bible in several places, not least the "All shall be well and all manner of thing shall be well" that translates *shalom* better than does the Vulgate's *recte* and the Wyclif Bible's "right." The Hebrew word for peace, Maria Boulding tells us, means far more than a truce amidst war, which is the sense of the Greek *irēnē*, the fleeting rainbow amidst storms, *shalom* being instead a totalizing of wellness, goodness, oneness, creation and Creator in harmony. One of the extant manuscripts Adam Easton once owned is Rabbi David Kimhi's *Sepher Miklol*. Kimhi wrote: "Jerome your translator erred in corrupting the text, 'The Lord said to my Lord, Sit at my right hand,'" of Psalm 110:1. Adam Easton explained that the phrase does not mean "right hand" literally, but "honoured." The author of *The Cloud of Unknowing* says the same thing. (This is one reason why it is possible he may be Adam Easton.) And Julian's text concurs. Earlier, Marguerite Porete had been burned at the stake in Paris, 1 June 1310, for proclaiming in *The Mirror of Simple Souls* things similar to those Julian would write. Later, Elizabeth Barton, who read the books of Birgitta of Sweden and Catherine of Siena and, perhaps, Julian of Norwich, at Syon Abbey, and was moved to write a great Book of Revelations modeled on theirs, when questioned whether the Son sat at the "right hand" of God the Father replied, "Nay it was not so, but One was before Any Other and One in Neither." For which she was hanged publicly on Tyburn, and beheaded, 20 April 1534.

A young Russian woman scholar, when translating Julian into Cyrillic, queried why Julian speaks of our time and God's time becoming one time. The reason for this is that in the Middle Ages time is seen as like a clock face, we on the outside having just a part of it, God at the center being all time, no past, no future, for all these are present at one and the same time. When we attain the center we are in that "oneness" of time with God that is eternity. This is stated in Augustine's *Confessions* XI and in Boethius' *Consolation of Philosophy*. In Judaism time is linear; in Hellenism it was believed the world was eternal and always would exist, not being created in time, not ending in apocalypse. Christianity blended the two time systems into this image of the circle and the center. Julian sees God in a point. It sometimes seems that Julian's great secret that God will do at the end of time will be to have time go backward, back to Adam, before the Fall, thus saving God's Word in all things, undoing all sin, as he tells her he will do. Julian also uses again and again the expression of God's knowing "without beginning," from "before any time," as knowing what shall be from before beginning, being there with grace and mercy in our prayer before we pray. Both she and Adam Easton speak of *presciencia*, forseeing, and of the need not to lose time, God's gift to us. The *Cloud of Unknowing* author says that God gives us one time, not two, and that we must use it well. Julian, the *Pearl* poet and the Gospel parable of the workers in the vineyard also explain that one day's prayer, or prayer in one's youth, may be enough to save one's soul.

Julian uses the word "kind" to mean nature, what is natural. And as is true in medieval theology, nature is of God, while sin is to act against nature. To be cruel and selfish and competitive, to be "red in tooth and claw," is to be against nature, unnatural. Somewhere between Julian's fourteenth century and our twenty-first, nature has been conceptually barbarized, mechanized, and violated. Indeed, Julian's text looks back to far earlier texts, from the dawn of history, from Babylon, from Egypt, from Rome, from before Christianity, all of which speak of the need to defend the weak against the strong, to be "kind," natural, nurturing, to others rather than to one's self, as the mark of civilization, of humankind, of the survival of the whole. Julian speaks of man and woman created in God's nurturing image. In this Julian's most obvious model is Hildegard of Bingen, whose final text, in a finely illuminated manuscript preserved in Lucca, the *Liber divinorum operum simplicis hominis,* speaks of the need for humankind to reverence nature as of God, not violating it, for health and wholeness, for the *shalom* of the creation. Julian's more modern and far more despairing counterpart is Mary Shelley writing *Frankenstein,* which is the *Showing of Love* reversed and turned inside out, the human de-natured, de-humanized, mechanized, a world of lonely, abusive cruelty.

IV. On *The Book of Margery Kempe* and the *Showing of Love*

When the learned, humble Julian was old and in her Norwich anchor-hold, around 1413–1415, at the time the Amherst Manuscript *Showing of Love* says it was being written, she was visited by another would-be anchoress, this one illiterate, traumatized, having books read to her, such as one about Marie de Oignies and one by Birgitta of Sweden, who had both, like her, been married. Margery Kempe was the mother of many children, only one of whom seems to have survived, and whose son and daughter-in-law, for her therapy, had her dictate her *Book of Margery Kempe.* Reading Margery's *Book* is like having a tape recorder in medieval Norwich brought from medieval Lynn, with the tape replayed in Lynn years later. For this reason, in this section we present the original surviving texts as they stand, rather than translating them, to give the readers of this translation as close as possible a sense of Julian's oral text, her spoken voice, her dialect. (For the manuscripts see Julian of Norwich, *Showing of Love,* ed. Sister Anna Maria Reynolds, c.p. and Julia Bolton Holloway [Florence: SISMEL, Edizioni del Galluzzo, 2001].)

Margery in *The Book of Margery Kempe* has her scribes explain to us (M, folio 21)

> & than sche was bodyn be owyr lord. for to gon to an ankres in the same Cyte which hyte Dame Jelyan. & so sche dede & schewyd hir the grace that god put in hir sowle of compunccyon contricyon swetnesse & devocyon compassyon with holy meditacyon & hy contemplacyon. & ful many holy spechys & dalyawns. that owyr Lord spak to hir sowle. and many wondirful reuelacyons whech sche schewyd to the ankres to wetyn yf ther were any deceyte in hem, for the ankres was expert in swech thynges & good cownsel cowd geuyn.

Julian's Amherst Manuscript concludes with an essay on the "Discerning of Spirits." Cardinal Adam Easton had a copy of Alfonso of

Jaén's *Epistola Solitarii* on Birgitta of Sweden, including the "Discerning of Spirits." Had Cardinal Easton instructed the Norwich anchoress, she would certainly have been as "expert" as Margery Kempe claims in the discerning of such spiritual matters and such revelatory showings.

Margery and Julian's conversation continues:

> The ankres, heryng the meruelyows goodnes of owyr lord, hyly thankyd god. with al hir hert. for thys vistacyon cownselung this creature to be obedyent. to the wyl of owyr lord god & fulfyllyn with al hir myghtys.
> whateuer he put in hir sowle yf it wer not ageyn the worshep of god & profyte of hir euyne cristen, for yf it were than it were nowt the mevyng of a good spyryte but rather of an euyl spyrit.

Julian's words to Margery echo the precepts of the *Cloud of Unknowing* author concerning the "Discerning of Spirits." That material had already been given in William Flete's *Remedies Against Temptations*, which similarly influenced Julian's *Showing of Love.* William Flete had left England in 1358 after writing that work to become the Augustinian hermit at Leccetto, associated with St. Catherine of Siena, whose *Dialogo* seems to have influenced Julian. In the passage we also hear Julian's own beloved phrase, "euyne cristen," and we can clearly recognize the echoes to the concluding section concerning the "Discernment of Spirits" in the Julian corpus unique to the Amherst Manuscript (Ⱶ114v-115), and which may perhaps be her last words:

> Alle dredes othere thann reuererente dredes. that er proferde to vs. thowgh thay comm vndere the coloure of halynes thay ere not so trewe. and hereby may thaye be knawenn and discerned. whilke is whilke. for this reuerente drede the mare it is hadde. the mare it softes and comfortes & pleses and restes and the false drede it travayles and tempestes & trubles than is this the remedye to knawe thamm bath & refuse the fals. righte as we walde do a wikkyd spiritte that schewed hym in liknes of a goode Angelle. for ryght as ane ille spyrit thowgh he comm vndere the coloure and the liknes of agoode angelle his daliaunce & his wirkynge thowgh he schewe neuer so fayre fyrst he travayles & tempes & trubles the persoun that he spekes with and lettes hym and lefes hym alle in unreste. And the mare that he commones with hym the mare he travayles hym. and the farthere is he fra pees. therfore it is goddes wille. and oure spede that we knawe thamm thus y sundure ffor god wille euer that we be sekere in luffe & peessabille & ristefulle

as he is to vs and ryght so of the same condicioun as he is to us so
wille he that we be to oure selfe. And to oure. Evencristenn. Amen.

Julian continues in her conversation with Margery, and is now reported
in direct speech:

> The holy gost meuyth neuyer a thing a-geyn charite &, yf he dede
> he were contraryows to hys owyn self for he is al charite. Also he
> meuyth a sowle to al chastenesse. for chast leuars be clepyd the
> temple of the holy gost [1 Cor 6:19]. & the holy gost makyth a
> sowle stabyl & stedfast in the rygth feyth & the rygth beleue. And
> a dubbyl man in sowle is euer vnstabyl. & vnstedfast in al hys
> weys. He that is euermor dowtyng. is lyke to the flood of the see.
> the wheche is mevyd & born a-bowte with the wynd, & that man is
> not lyche to receyuen the gyftys of god. What creature that hath
> thes tokenys he muste [M 21v] stedfastlych belevyn that the holy
> gost dwellyth in hys sowle. And mech more whan God visyteth a
> creature wyth terys of contrisyon deuosyon er compassyon. he
> may & owyth to leuyn that the holy gost is in hys sowle.

The image of the storm-tossed sea reflects that in the *Cloud of Unknowing* author's *A Pistle of Discretion of Stirings*, again a work on the
"Discerning of Spirits" (*EETS* 231:64.7-23).

Julian cites Saints Paul and Jerome to Margery:

> Seynt Powyl seyth that the Holy Gost Askyth for vs with morn-
> ingges & wepynges vnspekable. that is to seyn he makyth vs to
> askyn & preyn wyth mornyngges & wepynges so plentyvowsly.
> that the terys may not be nowmeryd [Rom 8:26]. Ther may non
> euyl spyrit geuyn thes tokenys, for Sanctum Jerom seyth that terys
> turmentyn more the Debylle than don the peynes of Helle.

Julian next discusses evil:

> god & the deuyl ben euermor contraryows & thei xal neuer dwellyn
> togedyr in on place. & the devyl hath no powyr in a mannys sowle.
> Holy wryt seyth that the sowle of a rytful man is the sete/seet of
> God. & so I trust, syster, that ye ben.

With that last comment, "& so I trust, syster, that ye ben," we realize
that we certainly are listening to reported speech and that Dame Julian
addressed Dame Margery, her "evyn cristen," even as "Sister." How-
ever, the discussion of evil in this conversation reminds one more of

William Flete's *Remedies Against Temptations* than it does of Julian's "sin as nought."

In this passage has Julian intended not "city," but "seat," or has Margery misheard the word? But perhaps Julian deliberately plays upon the likeness of the two words. She may be using the concept expressed throughout Luke 14 where guests need to exercise humility to enter the kingdom of God, a kingdom that is among us.

Apart from the Hilton and Julian texts in the Westminster Manuscript making this same point are other texts associated with Julian, among them Norwich Castle Manuscript, fol. 78v:

> ¶ If we weel desyre to been in his companye thanne loue hym with al oure soule the wiche is ordeyned to been goddis temple goddis hous goddis see ¶ Quia iusti sedes est sapiencie. ffor as seith holy write the soule of the rytful man or womman is the see & dwelling of endeles wisdom that is goddis sone swete ihc If we been besy & doon our deuer to fulfille the wil of god & his pleasaunce thanne loue we hym wit al our myte.

Likewise John Whiterig, fellow student with Adam Easton at Oxford, then hermit on Farne Island, uses this passage, "Anima iusti sedes est sapiencie," in *Contemplating the Crucifixion*, deriving it from Prov 10:25b (cf. Gregory, *Hom. XXXVIII in Evang.*, Migne, *PL* 76, 1282).

Julian's theology presents this marvelously wise image of the city in the soul, Christ its king. Margery's text had emphasized the City of Norwich with its inspired and inspiring anchoress:

> & than sche was bodyn be owyr lord. for to gon to an ankres in the same Cyte which hyte Dame Jelyan'.

In Julian's day Norwich was the second-largest city in England, its cathedral being rebuilt during her lifetime in Gothic style. We see it imaged as Hagia Sophia within Constantinople in the Luttrell Psalter. Spiritually, the period was inspiring magnificent church art and architecture—and Julian's *Showing*. The Middle Ages, shaped by Plato and Revelation and St. Augustine, saw as the task of the City of Man to shape itself into the City of God, to have the care not only of bodies but of souls. Today when we think of Norwich it is the soaring cathedral of the Holy and Undivided Trinity and the humble anchorhold in St. Julian's Alley and its anchoress that come to mind. Let us leap forward to George Eliot writing on Coventry and the Reform Act in her *Middlemarch*, reflecting back to Plato and his *Republic:*

1st. Gent. An ancient land in ancient oracles is called "law-thirsty." All the struggle there was after order and a perfect rule. Pray, where lie such lands now?

2nd Gent. Why, where they lay of old—in human souls.

Interestingly, this phrasing concerning the soul as a city is closer to that of the Sixteenth Showing in the 1393/1580 Paris Manuscript and the 1413/1450s Amherst Manuscript (Ꝑ143v-145v; Ⱨ112), which both give vestiges of the Lord and the Servant Parable, than it is to the earlier version, the Fourteenth Showing, present in the Westminster and Paris Manuscripts (Ⱳ101-102v; Ꝑ116-119).

Bot than lefte I Stylle wakande and than owre lorde openedde my gastely eyenn & schewyd me my saule in myddys of my herte. I sawe my saule swa large as it ware a kyngdome And be the condicions that I sawe therin. me thought it was awirschipfulle Cite. In myddys of this Cite Sittes oure lorde Jhesu verraye god & verray mann a fayre persoune and of large stature wyrschipfulle. hiest lorde. And I sawe hym cledde Solemplye in wyrschippes. he sittes in the saule euenn ryght in pees & reste. And he rewles & gemes heuenn & erthe. and alle that is. the manhede with the godhede sittis in reste. And the godhede rewles & gemes with owtynn any instrumente or besynes. And my saule blisfullye occupyed with the godhede. that is Sufferaynn myght. Sufferayne. Wisdomme Sufferayne goodnesse. The place that Jhesu takes in oure saule. he schalle neuer remove it with owtynn ende. for in vs is his haymelyeste hame. & maste lykynge to hym to dwelle in this was adelectabille syght. & a restefulle. for it is so in trowth with owtenn ende. And the behaldynge of this whiles we ere here es fulle plesaunde to god and fulle grete spede to vs. And the saule that thus behaldys it: makys it lyke to hym that is behaldene and anes in reste & in pees and this was asingulere ioye & Ablis to me. that I sawe hym sitte for the behaldynge of this sittynge. schewed to me sikernes of his endelesse dwellynge.

This can be compared to the 1368/1500s Westminster Manuscript's more subtle account concerning Julian's vision of the Kingdom of Heaven, the City of God, within one's own soul (Ⱳ 101-102v), whose words, "God is nearer to us than our own soul," had already been spoken by Angela of Foligno:

God is nerer to vs. than owre owne soule. for he is grounde in whom
oure soule stondyth. and he is mene that kepith the substance &
the sensualyte togeder so that it shall neuer depart. for oure soule
syttith in god. in verey reste. and oure soule standith in god in sure
strength. & oure soule is kyndely rooted in god. in endelesse loue.
& therfore yf we wyll haue knowynge of oure soule. & communynge & daliance therwith: It behouyth to seke into oure lord god in
whom it is enclosyd. And annentis oure substance it may ryght-
fully be called our soule. and anentis our sensualite it may ryght-
full be called our soule. and that is by the onyng that it hath in god.
That wurshypfull cite that our lord ihesu syttith in. it is our sensualite. in whiche he is enclosed. and our kyndely substance is
beclosyd in ihesu criste. with the blessed soule of criste syttyng in
reste in the godhed. And I sawe ful surely that it behouyth nedis
that we shall be in longynge and in penance. into the tyme that we
be led so depe in to god that we may verely & truely know oure
owne soule. And sothly I saw that in to thys high depenes oure
lorde hym selfe ledith vs in the same loue that he made vs. and in
the same loue that he bought vs. bi his mercy & grace through
vertue of his blessed passion. And not withstondyng all this we
may neuer comme to the full knowyng of god. tyll we first know
clerely oure owne soule. ffor into the tyme that it be in the ffull
myghtis we may not be all full holy. and that is that oure sensualite. by the vertue of cristis passion be brought up into the
substance with all the profitis of oure tribulacion that oure lorde
shall make vs to gete by mercy & grace.

The Paris Manuscript gives first the Westminster Manuscript version as part of the Fourteenth Showing, greatly expanding it, while
noting that it is to be spoken of again later in the Sixteenth Showing
(P116-119). In that Sixteenth Showing it is given just as in the Amherst
Manuscript, where it appears to be in the form of Julian's consolatory
sermon for those who would have felt lost and bewildered by the
subtlety of the earlier, far more precocious account (P144-145). While
W101v-102v and P116-119 are now excised from the Amherst text, elements can still be traced in Julian's words to Margery, especially where
they all speak of "communynge & daliance therwith" (W101-101v),
"comenyng and dalyance therwith" (P118v.5-6), and Margery's use of
these same words at the conclusion of her soul talk with Julian: "the
holy dalyawns that the ankres & this creature haddyn be comownyng
in the lofe of owyr lord Jhesu crist."

Julian continues:

> "I prey god grawnt yow perseuerawns. Settyth al yore trust in god.
> & feryth not the langage of the world. for the more despyte schame
> & repref that ye haue in the world the more is yowr meryte in the
> sygth of god. Pacyens is necessary vnto yow. for in that schal ye
> kepyn yore sowle."

V. On the *Showing of Love*'s Manuscripts

Widespread destruction of Julian's manuscripts of the *Showing of Love* would have occurred first under the persecution of the Lollards. Then even more such manuscripts and printed books would have been destroyed under the persecution of the Catholics. Because of the Reformation all but one, the Amherst Manuscript (Ⱶ), of Julian's surviving manuscripts of the *Showing of Love* came to be outside of England. Today only one remains abroad, the Paris Manuscript (Ꝑ). There may still be undiscovered Julian manuscripts in Flemish or Dutch libraries, which were the exemplars to Sloane and Paris. It would be splendid if these could be discovered. That all these Julian of Norwich *Showing of Love* manuscripts have Brigittine or Benedictine connections argues for the patronage of her work by Adam Easton.

The Westminster Cathedral Manuscript (Ⱳ)

The Westminster Cathedral Manuscript was, according to its dialect and script, written out at the Brigittine Syon Abbey by a Brigittine nun there, around 1450. She had access to other manuscripts of the *Showing of Love*, for her text is carefully corrected against them. The manuscript begins with works from Walter Hilton, two Psalm commentaries, and excerpts from *The Ladder of Perfection*, a work Hilton originally wrote to guide an anchoress' contemplation, followed by a preliminary or abbreviated version of Julian of Norwich's *Showing of Love*. It is written on parchment in a beautiful hand, within rulings on the small folios, and the texts begin with initial capitals in blue with red penwork, that of Julian using the {O of the "Great O Antiphon," said by the Virgin to her yet unborn child in Advent, "O Sapientia." In this Julian's text imitates and recalls the image used by Marguerite Porete of her book, *The Mirror of Simple Souls,* as an engendering within her by God. The Amherst

Manuscript with Julian's Short Text *Showing of Love* gives the complete text of Porete's book, anonymously translated into Middle English, at its folios 137-225.

Syon Abbey had to go into exile, first under Henry VIII, then again under Elizabeth I. At the Dissolution some of its nuns were forced to marry. On the final folio of the Westminster Manuscript are pen trials giving the names of members of the Lowe family, who also had owned a Syon Abbey Psalter now in Edinburgh in which the birth of a daughter, "Elinor Mounse Lowe," is recorded on the vigil of the feast of the Holy Innocents, with a prayer that God make her a good woman. Syon Abbey was first in exile in the Low Countries, then at Rouen, finally making its way to Lisbon. There Sister Rose Lowe saved the community from extinction and it was possibly she who in 1821 gave this manuscript to Bishop James Bramston, who had studied theology at the English College in Lisbon, for it has his bookplate and his annotations calculating the manuscript's age, as written in "1368," because at the bottom of the manuscript's first folio is the number "1368," though the manuscript itself is clearly later than that date. Perhaps this was meant to indicate that the original exemplar was written in 1368. It appears to desire to preserve what would have been the version of the *Showing of Love* that Julian could have written when she was twenty-five years of age and five years before the seeming "deathbed" visions of 1373, for it contains none of these. The manuscript was rebound in 1821, with the date "1368" stamped on the spine.

The Paris, Bibliothèque Nationale, Anglais 40 Manuscript ($\mathcal{P}$)

Today this is the only known manuscript of Julian of Norwich's *Showing of Love* that is still outside England. The Paris Manuscript gives the complete Long Text written out circa 1580 on Flemish paper by a Brigittine nun in exile there. It is copying a now-lost Tudor manuscript prepared for printing by Syon Abbey just prior to the beheading of Thomas More and the dissolution of the monasteries. The majority of Julian manuscripts present Christ's words to her in larger letters than the rest of the text, copying the practice one sees in Adam Easton's manuscript in Hebrew of Rabbi David Kimhi's *Sepher Miklol*. But this would have been a printer's headache, and here the scribe instead uses rubrication in red of the chapter headings, the paragraph signs ¶, and Christ's words to Julian. These conventions were used in sacred books from the beginning of literacy, for instance in the Egyptian *Book of the Dead,* as well as in Christian prayerbooks and in red letter Bibles. The beginning letter of each chapter of the Paris *Showing of Love* is capitalized in blue. This translation published by The Liturgical Press replicates these conventions from (ꝗ), though replacing the blue capitals with large initial letters in red.

Syon Abbey had to go into exile twice. During the second exile the poverty of the nuns became so great that they sent several of the younger sisters in disguise back to England to raise funds and to seek to have books printed for the English mission, one of these being Walter Hilton's *Ladder of Perfection* and another, perhaps, Julian of Norwich's *Showing of Love.* These sisters braved imprisonment and death. Under Henry VIII several Syon Sisters had continued to live their life of contemplative prayer in the house of a member of one of their families, the damp, moated Lyford Grange. The sisters returned there, then fled when several of the Recusants from the Grange were imprisoned, including members of the Lowe family, which owned ꝗ. Several had already died in Reading Prison. One sister, Elizabeth Saunders, was captured, and her books with her, at Alton; she was questioned by the Anglican Bishop of Winchester, who then imprisoned her in Winchester Castle, seizing the "certaine lewde and forbidden bokes" from her, likely the Tudor exemplar of Julian of Norwich's *Showing of Love* among them. Another sister, Marie Champney, died of tuberculosis in London, on her deathbed seeking the printing of books, including Walter Hilton's *Ladder of Perfection.*

While these sisters were in England, Syon Abbey itself moved from the dangers of the Low Countries to similar dangers in Rouen, France, the sisters eventually making their way from there to Lisbon in Portugal by ship with their possessions in five crates and a cask. They brought with them the marble gatepost of Syon Abbey, sculpted with the instruments of the Passion, on which part of Richard Reynolds' quartered body had been exposed. They have it still, now in their chapel in Devon. But they had to leave behind this manuscript of Julian of Norwich's *Showing of Love.* It instead entered the great library of the Bigot family in Rouen, which was eventually purchased for the King's Library in Paris, arriving there too late for consultation by Serenus Cressy for his 1670 edition of the *Revelations of Divine Love.* He must have used either this manuscript's Tudor exemplar or its Elizabethan twin copy.

This text notes internally that it was the edition formed by Julian twenty years after her vision, therefore originally written in 1393, likely revising the version found in Sloane. It has removed from itself the editorializing chapter headings and colophon of the Sloane manuscripts, seeming to consider them unnecessary.

The British Library Sloane Manuscripts 3701 and 2499 (S)

There are two further manuscripts of the Long Text of Julian of Norwich's *Showing of Love*. The first of these, Sloane 3701, was copied out from a now lost exemplar written probably in the hand of Julian herself, and which was in her Norwich dialect, the copy being made at Cambrai, circa 1650, on Flemish paper, by English Benedictine nuns in exile there. Sloane 3701 modernizes the text. The English Benedictines at Cambrai had Dom Augustine Baker, O.S.B., as spiritual director; he encouraged them in their reading and preserving of medieval contemplative texts, such as Walter Hilton, the *Cloud of Unknowing* author, and Julian of Norwich. Then jealousy arose, the monks desiring to confiscate and prohibit the nuns' now extensive contemplative library. So Cambrai Abbey, in a burst of copying, created an insurance library and even founded a daughter house especially for it, in 1651, sending some of their nuns to Paris with these precious copies, at least two, perhaps more, of Julian of Norwich's *Showing of Love* among them. In that burst of copying Dame Clementia Cary, who had been maid in waiting to Queen Henrietta Maria, returned to the exemplar for Sloane 3701 and now copied its medieval dialect exactly, preserving its forms. She was meticulously editing a fourteenth-century work in the seventeenth century. Her manuscript is the hastily-written Sloane 2499. Her ecstatic comments, made during her initial reading of the text, are found in the margins of Sloane 3701, which clearly preceded Sloane 2499 also in the dating of its watermarks. Dom Serenus Cressy, O.S.B., the chaplain to the Paris daughter house, then had printed the first edition of Julian of Norwich's *Revelations of Divine Love* in 1670, using as base text the twin or exemplar of P and giving marginal collations derived from these fine S manuscripts.

The S manuscripts differ from P in having chapter headings, from their wording clearly written by an editor during Julian's lifetime, which P lacks, given here in gray. They also have a colophon echoing that to the Middle English manuscripts of Marguerite Porete's *Mirror of Simple Souls,* (of which there are three, one of these actually being with Julian's *Showing of Love* in the Amherst Manuscript), and those to the works of the author of *The Cloud of Unknowing*. Two other Benedictine nuns, Dame Barbara Constable of Cambrai in the Upholland Manuscript (Ⅱ) and Dame Bridget More (descendant of Thomas More) of Paris in the Dame Margaret Gascoigne Manuscript (Ϭ), copied out excerpts from Julian's *Showing*. We even have portraits of these two scribes in their Benedictine garb. Cambrai was finally to return from exile at the Revolution and become Stanbrook Abbey, Paris likewise becoming Colwich Abbey —but not before both abbeys were imprisoned and the religious at risk of being guillotined, Cambrai's nuns coming home to England in the clothing of their dead fellow prisoners, the Carmelites, who had gone to the scaffold bravely singing "Salve Regina," the day of Our Lady of Carmel, 16 July 1794.

This Sloane text notes internally that it is the edition formed fifteen years after Julian's vision, therefore written in 1388. It presents much editorializing, in the form of the table of contents, the chapter headings and the colophon, written by another, given here in gray, and appears to have been written under the direction of a learned and appreciative cleric.

The Amherst Manuscript, British Library Additional 37,790 (Ⱶ)

In the Paris and Sloane Manuscripts' Long Text Julian states that she yearns to perform her *Book* differently, as if she rebelled against the pigeonholing of fifteen "Showings" and chapters and interminable cross-references and elitist colophons, copying the conventions of the multiply-edited Brigittine *Revelationes*. Already the Paris Manuscript had begun the process in ignoring the editorializing chapter descriptions and colophon. Then, when Julian was seventy, in 1413, the text was rewritten, becoming the Amherst Manuscript's Short Text, as if the author were witnessing and writing a legal document rather than a theological treatise, now omitting much of her biblical translation and adaptation into English while keeping and even expanding on the physical details of the "deathbed" vision of very many years before. Under life-threatening constraints she crystallizes her text and her theology, and justifies her writing of it. Her scribe, by his dialect, is from Lincolnshire, a Carmelite, and responsible also for other fine manuscripts for women contemplatives. He is the only male scribe of all seven extant Julian of Norwich *Showing of Love* manuscripts. Like Westminster and Paris, the manuscript uses capitals in blue, ornamented with red quill work, dividing the text into sections that do not always correspond to the Long Text's now abandoned structure of sixteen Showings. It is these capital letters, rather than numbers, that Julian seems to prefer for her memory system for her manuscripts. Moreover, in Amherst another hand than its scribe has restored the eye-skipped lines that scribe omitted. It is a hand that reminds one of that in the Norwich Castle manuscript, square and Tudor-like, though likewise written at the opening of the fifteenth century, during Julian's lifetime and evocative of the hand of the late Adam Easton. It is possible that these two manuscripts contain Julian's own handwriting.

This text in the Amherst manuscript clearly states internally that it was being written in 1413 and during Julian's lifetime.

VI. On This Composite Edition and Translation

Most modern editions and translations transform a manuscript text into something new and strange, like a black-and-white photograph of what once was in reds and blues and with gold leaf upon purple, reducing it from its former glory and memorability into something ordinary and easy to forget. This translation, based on the definitive edition by Sister Anna Maria Reynolds, C.P. and Julia Bolton Holloway, published by SISMEL, Edizioni del Galluzzo, Florence, 2001 (ISBN 88-8450-095-8), instead seeks to replicate as far as possible that original glory of Julian's manuscripts, indeed to present what Syon Abbey's nuns had twice sought to have printed in England, under Henry VIII and under Elizabeth I, having prepared the manuscript for the press as we see it in the Paris Manuscript. The SISMEL edition gives separate translations of Westminster (𝖂), Paris (𝖕), and Amherst (𝕳), while this translation presents a composite based on Sloane (𝕾) but showing the important variants to that text. The rubrication is that in the Paris Manuscript (𝖕) (the ¶ a convenient way then to save parchment and now to save paper); the pagination is that in the Sloane Manuscript (𝕾), indicated by the symbol ▨▧▨; the punctuation follows the clues given in the various manuscripts, as these demonstrate Julian's cadenced English; the ornamented capitals in Westminster and Amherst are given so: {O and those in Paris so: 𝕳. Julian and/or her scribes capitalized temporal titles, such as Church (but not its adjective, holy), King, Lord, etc., but usually not spiritual ones, "god, father, brother, maiden, mother." The variants given use (𝖂𝕾𝖕𝕳𝕲𝖀) to signify which parts of the texts are from the Westminster, Sloane, Paris, Amherst, Gascoigne, and Upholland manuscripts. This translation functions as a platform from which it becomes possible to see the whole while showing the layering of texts throughout the many years of Julian's lifework.

Donald Frame once so edited and translated Montaigne's *Essays*, showing the layers of text and their accretions through time as the *Essays* went into printing upon printing. Augustine's *Confessions* and Samuel Beckett's *Krapp's Last Tape* similarly are self-consciously aware of the stages of the author's life enfolded into the author's text. The same may be seen here, where we read all Julian's surviving texts in translation simultaneously. Let us hypothesize that the Westminster Cathedral (𝖂) Manuscript attempted to show what Julian's original text might have been in 1368, when she was twenty-five, before her "deathbed" vision, that the Sloane (𝖲) and Paris (𝖯) manuscripts give her 1373 vision at thirty as frame to her 1368 theology and as initially written down in 1388–93, when she was fifty, and the Amherst (𝕳) Manuscript written by a scribe whom she perhaps corrects, in 1413, when she was seventy, in the face of Arundel's draconian censorship, her Amherst text nevertheless crystallizing her teaching on prayer for all her even-Christians, men and women both. All three versions importantly include the vision of the hazelnut, of all that is, in Julian's hand and in ours, of God's city in Julian's and our soul, and of her desire to die young to be soon with God, as the heart of Julian's contemplation. Jesus as Mother is in Westminster, Sloane, and Paris (𝖂𝖲𝖯), but censored from Amherst (𝕳). The Parable of the Lord and the Servant, possibly allegorically about Adam Easton's torture and imprisonment by Pope Urban VI, is only present in the Sloane and Paris Long Texts. The "deathbed" vision of 1373 is given in Sloane, Paris and Amherst, in this last being given greater self-referential detail, as if for a witnessed legal document, justifying her writing in the face of Arundel's death-dealing censorship and crystallizing her theology. Such a document would have been of use after her death for canonization purposes. Similar material had been compiled for the attempted canonization of the hermit Richard Rolle. To these collations are also added the fragments written out in Cambrai in the Margaret Gascoigne/Bridget More Manuscript (𝕲) and the Barbara Constable Upholland Manuscript (𝖀). The letters (𝕸) and (𝕹) refer to passages found also in the Book of Margery Kempe manuscript and the Norwich Castle manuscript.

I have sought in this composite translation to remain as faithful to Julian's English as is possible. Both T. S. Eliot and Thomas Merton have highly praised her writing. The manuscripts represent different dialects,

Sloane being that of Julian's own Norwich, Amherst that of the neighbouring Lincoln, Westminster and Paris being the London dialect. I have regularized these to modern standard English. Grammar has shifted between her day and ours. Verbs and their agreement with nouns in Julian's text can differ from our practices. The eighteenth century, on the model of logic, abolished the double negative as positive, requiring either one or the other, but not both. Consequently these are pruned to modern usage. In order to preserve the nature of Julian's original text, words are translated usually into modern equivalents where they are no longer current coin, but sometimes the original word is employed to teach us what it was. We have one word for "truly," while Julian has three, "sothly, verily, truly." Usually I give our modern word, "truly," but at times I employ her medieval words. I have retained her "holy Ghost" and "ghostly" for "Spirit" and "spiritual." Her admiring male editor, who writes the Table of Contents, the chapter headings, and the elitist colophon, likes Latin words, such as "Revelations," while Julian prefers Anglo-Saxon ones, like "Showing." The manuscripts give "blissful, blessedful" as interchangeable one with the other. I have Americanized some spelling, but kept her English "colour" and "honour."

This list gives words this translation sometimes changes, sometimes retains:

abide = wait, stay
anon = soon
as farforth = as much as
Asseth = satisfaction, reparation, assay
attemyd = humbled, avisement, attention
be = by
behove = need
beseek = pray, beseech
bliss = bless
bolned = swollen
buxom = pliant, obedient, humble
cheer = expression, mood
creature = a being created by God
demed = judged
depart = separate
example = parable
full = most
Ghost = Spirit

grevid = pregnant
hende = gracious
homely = friendly, familiar
kind = nature
largesse = generosity
learning = teaching
leve = believe (similar to Middle
    English words for leave and live)
let = stop, hinder
like = please, delight
manner = way, kind
meddle = mixed
mede = reward
mind = think, contemplate, memory
nought = nothing
onde = wind, breath
one = unite
particular = special

privy = secret	that = who
reward = regard	the, thou = you
rood = cross	Uprising = Resurrection
securely = surely	verily = truly
Showing = Revelation	wax = grow
skillful = expert, wise	wele = weal, wellness, well being
sothly = truly	wened = believed, thought
speed = help, assist, benefit	willfully = willingly
stint = cease, stop	wist = knew
suffer = allow, permit	wonyng = home, dwelling
swemful = grief	worship = honour, reverence
swithe = sudden	wroth = to be angry, wrathful

Though the list alphabetically ends with the word "wroth," Julian tells us that in God there is no wrath. Nevertheless, her *Showing of Love* elicited much wrath and was censored and hidden for centuries, first as a Lollard text, then as Catholic. In her writing she seeks to reconcile the theologies of Easton and Wyclif; today she would seek to reconcile men and women, Jew and Christian, Ireland and England, Rome and Canterbury. We need her Apocalypse, her Revelation, her *Showing of Love* more than ever. Reading her words, let us give thanks for the centuries of women and men in exile, in prison, awaiting execution, suffering from burning at the stake, drawing, hanging and quartering, and guillotining, who, in prayer to God, preserved the *Showing of Love* for us. It is a story of courage and consolation, reminding us that God is Father and Mother both, of might, of wisdom, of love, cherishing and nourishing all, despising nothing God has made. It reminds us that God is in smallness as in greatness, in women as in men, in children as in the grown, in seeds and their genetic codes, in atoms and their molecular structures, present as the sacred ABC in all things, from which bodies and books are born, "that all manner of thing shall be well." For this *Showing of Love* you now hold in your hand is Julian's book and God's book, we mirroring Eve (whom Julian never names) and Adam, Mary and Jesus, in whom we are all contained.

"O Sapientia"
Florence, 2002

Julian of Norwich

SHOWING OF LOVE

𝕎 = Westminster Cathedral Manuscript, On Loan, Westminster Abbey, '1368'/circa 1450/1500, London Dialect, Syon Abbey, London/Lisbon

𝕊 = Sloane, British Library, Sloane Manuscripts 2499, 3705, '1387–1393'/1650–1670, Norwich Dialect, Cambrai/Paris

𝕡 = Paris, Bibliothèque Nationale, anglais 40, Manuscript, '1387–1393'/circa 1580, London Dialect, Syon-in-Exile

ℍ = Amherst, British Library, Amherst Manuscript, Additional 37,790, '1413'/1413–1435, Lincoln Dialect, Lincoln Carmel, Sheen/Syon

𝔾 = Margaret Gascoigne Manuscript, Scribe, Bridget More, St. Mary's Abbey, Colwich, H18, Cambrai/Paris/Colwich

𝕌 = Upholland Fragment Manuscript, Scribe, Barbara Constable, Cambrai/Upholland

𝕄 = The Book of Margery Kempe, British Library, Aditional 61,823, Lynn Dialect, Lynn/Mount Grace Priory

ℕ = Norwich Castle Manuscript, 158.926/4g.5, Norwich Dialect

(S) Revelations to one who could not read a letter. Anno Domini 1373.
(p) Here Begins the First Chapter (Sp)

This is a Revelation of Love that Jesus Christ, our endless bliss, made in Sixteen Showings, of which ¶ The First Showing is of his precious crowning with thorns. And therein was comprehended and specified the Trinity with the Incarnation and Unity between God and man's soul with many fair Showings of endless wisdom and teachings of love, in which all the Showings that follow be grounded and oned. ¶ The Second Showing is the discolouring of his fair face in tokening of his dearworthy Passion. ¶ The Third Showing is that our Lord God, all mighty, all wisdom, all love, right as truly as he has made every thing that is, so truly he does and works all things that are done. ¶ The Fourth Showing is the scourging of his tender Body with plenteous shedding of his blood. ¶ The Fifth Showing is that the fiend is overcome by the precious Passion of Christ. ¶ The Sixth Showing is the worshipful thanking of our Lord God in which he rewards his blessed servants in heaven. ¶ The Seventh Showing is often feeling of weal and woe. Feeling of well-being is gracious touching and lightening, with true sureness of endless joy. The feeling of woe is temptation by heaviness and irksomeness of our fleshly living with ghostly understanding that we are kept so surely in love, in woe as in wellness, by the goodness of God. ¶ The Eighth Showing is the last pains of Christ and his cruel dying. ¶ The Ninth Showing is of the liking which is in the blessed Trinity of the hard Passion of Christ and his rueful dying in which joy and liking he will we be solaced and mirthed with him till we come to the fullness of heaven. ¶ The Tenth Showing is our Lord Jesus shows in love his blissful heart even cloven in two enjoying. ¶ The Eleventh Showing is a high ghostly Showing of his dearworthy Mother. ¶ The Twelfth Showing is that our Lord is most worthy being. ¶ The Thirteenth Showing is that our Lord God wills that we have great regard to all the deeds that he has done in the great nobleness of making all things and of the excellency of ▨▨▨ making man who is above all his works, and of the precious amends that he has made for man's sin, turning all our blame into endless worship, where also our Lord says, "Behold and see, for by the same might, wisdom and goodness, I shall make well all that is not well and you shall see it." And in this he wills we keep us in the faith and truth of holy Church, not willing to know his secrets now, but only as it belongs to us in this life. ¶ The Fourteenth Showing is that our Lord is ground of our prayer. Herein were seen two properties: that one is rightful prayer, that other is secure trust, which he wills both be alike large. And thus our prayer delights him and he of his goodness fulfills it. ¶ The Fifteenth Showing is that we shall suddenly be taken from all our pain and from all our woe, and of his goodness we shall come up above where we shall have our Lord Jesus to our reward and be fulfilled of joy and bliss in heaven. ¶ The Sixteenth Showing is that the blessedful Trinity, our Maker in Christ Jesus our Saviour, endlessly dwells in our soul, worshipfully ruling and giving all things, us mightily and wisely saving and keeping for love, and we shall not be overcome by our enemy.

(S) Of the time of these Revelations, and how she asked three petitions. (Sp) The Second Chapter.

This Revelation was made to a simple creature who knew no letter, the year of our Lord 1373 the (S) eighth (p) thirteenth (Sp) day of May, which creature had desired before three gifts of God. (A)

{ Here is a vision showed by the goodness of God to a devout woman, and her name is Julian, who is a recluse at Norwich and is living yet in this year of our Lord 1413. In which vision are very many comfortable and most stirring words to all those who desire to be Christ's lovers.

{ I desired three graces by the gift of God. (SpA) ¶ The first was mind of his Passion. ¶ The second was bodily sickness in youth at thirty years of age. ¶ The third was to have of God's gift three wounds. As in the first, I thought I had some feeling in the Passion of Christ. But yet I desired more by the grace of God. I thought I would have been that time with Mary Magdalen and with others who were Christ's lovers, that I might have seen bodily the Passion that our Lord suffered for me, that I might have suffered with him as others did who loved him, (A) notwithstanding that I believed solemnly all the pains of Christ as holy Church shows and teaches and also the paintings of Crucifixes that are made by the grace of God after the teaching of holy Church to the likeness of Christ's Passion as much as man's knowledge may reach. Notwithstanding all this true belief, (Sp) therefore I desired a bodily sight wherein I might have more knowledge of the bodily pains of our Saviour, and of the compassion of our Lady and of all his true lovers who saw that time his pains, for I would be one of them and suffer with him. I never desired any other sight or Showing of God till the soul were departed from the body. (SⱣꞍ) The cause of this petition was that after the Showing I should have the more true mind in the Passion of Christ. The second came to my mind with contrition freely desiring of God's gift, that sickness so hard as to the death that I might in that sickness undergo all my rites of holy Church, myself believing that I should die, and that all creatures might suppose the same who saw me, for I would have no kind of comfort of earthly life. In this sickness I desired to have all kinds of pains bodily and ghostly that I should have if I should die, with all the dreads and tempests of the fiends, except the outpassing of the soul. And this I meant for I would be purged by the mercy of God, and after live more to the worship of God, because of that sickness, and that for the more aid in my death, for I desired to be soon with my God. ¶ These two desires, of the Passion and the sickness, I desired with a condition, saying thus, "Lord, you know what I would, if it be your will that I have it, (Ꞁ) grant it me, (SⱣꞍ) and if it be not your will, good Lord, be not displeased, for I will nought but as you will." ¶ For the third, by the grace of God and teaching of holy Church, (Ꞁ) I heard a man tell of holy Church the story of <u>St Cecilia</u>. In the which Showing I understood she had three wounds with a sword, in the neck, from which she pined to the death. By the stirring of this, (SⱣꞍ) I conceived a mighty desire, to receive, three wounds in my life, that is to say, the wound of true contrition, the wound of natural compassion, and the wound of wilful longing to God. And all this last petition I asked without any condition. These two foresaid desires passed from my mind, and the third dwelled with me continually.

❦

(S) Of the sickness obtained of God by petition. (SⱣ) The Third Chapter. (SⱣꞍ)

{Ꞁ}nd when I was thirty (SⱣ) years (Ꞁ) winter (SⱣꞍ) old and a half, God sent me a bodily sickness in which I lay three days and three nights, and on the fourth night I took all my rites of holy

4 Church and thought not to have lived until day. And ▨ after this I
langoured a further two days and two nights. And on the third night,
I believed often times to have passed, and so believed they who were
with me, and in youth. Yet I thought it great grief to die, but I wanted to
live for nothing that was on earth, nor for any pain that I feared. For
I trusted in God of his mercy, but it was to have lived that I might have
loved God better and for longer time, that I might have the more knowing and loving of God in the bliss of heaven. ¶ For I thought all the time
that I had lived here, so little and so short in regard of that endless bliss,
I thought nothing. Wherefore I thought, "Good Lord, may my living no
longer be to your worship." ¶ And I understood by my reason and by
my feeling of my pains that I should die, and I assented fully with all
the will of my heart to be at God's will. ¶ Thus I endured till day and by
then my body was dead from the midst downwards as to my feeling.
Then was I stirred to be set upright, propped up with help, (Ħ) leaning
with cloths to my head, (SƿĦ) to have more freedom of my heart to
be at God's will, and thinking on God while my life would last. ¶ (Ħ)
And they who were with me sent for the Parson, my Curate (SƿĦ) to
be at my ending and by the time he came I had set my eyes and might
not speak. (Ħ) He came and a child with him and brought a cross. The
Parson (SƿĦ) set the Cross before my face and said, (Ħ) "Daughter,
(SƿĦ) I have brought you the image of your Saviour. Look upon it
and comfort yourself with it, (Ħ) in reverence of him who died for you
and me." (SƿĦ) I thought I was well, for my eyes were set up right-
ward into heaven, where I trusted to come by the mercy of God. ¶ But
nevertheless I assented to set my eyes in the face of the Crucifix, if I
might, and so I did. For I thought I might longer endure (Ħ) to the time
of my ending (SƿĦ) to look even forth than right up. After this my
sight began to fail and it was all dark about me in the chamber, (Ħ) and
murky (SƿĦ) as it had been night, save in the image of the Cross
wheren I beheld a common light, and I knew not how. All that was
5 beside the Cross was ugly to me as if it had ▨ been much occupied
with the fiends. ¶ After this the other part of my body began to die so
much that scarcely I had any feeling. My hands fell down on either
side. And also from weakness my head settled to one side. The most
pain I felt was with shortness of breath and failing of life. ¶ And then I
believed truly I would die. And in this suddenly all my pain was taken
from me and I was as hale and namely in the other part of my body
as ever I was before (Ħ) or after. (SƿĦ) I marveled at this sudden
change, for I thought it was a privy working of God, and not of nature,

and yet by the feeling of this ease I trusted never the more to live. Nor was this feeling of ease really comfort to me, for I thought I had rather be delivered from this world. ¶ (ᚻ)

{ᚻ}nd (ᛋᛈᚻ) came suddenly to my mind that I should desire the second wound of our Lord's gracious gift, (ᚻ) and of his grace, (ᛋᛈᚻ) that my body might be fulfilled with mind and feeling of his blessed Passion. For I would that his pains were my pains, with compassion and afterward longing to God. This I thought that I might with his grace have the wounds that I had before desired. But in this I desired never bodily sight nor any Showing of God, but compassion as, a natural soul might have with our Lord Jesus who for love would have been a mortal man, and therefore I desired to suffer with him. (ᛋᛈ)

The First Revelation. (ᛋ) Here Begins the First Revelation of the precious crowning of Christ, etc., in the First Chapter, and how God fulfills the heart with most joy and of his great meekness, and how the sight of the Passion of Christ is sufficient strength against all temptations of the fiends and of the great excellency and humility of the blessed Virgin Mary. (ᛋᛈ) The Fourth Chapter.

{ᚻ}nd in this suddenly I saw the red blood trickling down from under the Garland, hot and freshly and right plenteously, as it were in the time of his Passion that the garland of thorns was (ᛋᛈ) pressed (ᚻ) thrust (ᛋᛈᚻ) on his blessed head. Right so, both God and Man, the same who suffered thus for me. I conceived truly and mightily, that it was he himself who showed it to me without any intermediary. ¶ And in ⟨⟩ the same Showing suddenly the Trinity fulfilled my heart most of joy, and so I understood it shall be in heaven without end to all who shall come there. For the Trinity is God. God is the Trinity. The Trinity is our Maker and keeper, the Trinity is our everlasting lover, everlasting joy and bliss by our Lord Jesus Christ. And this was showed in the First Showing and in all, for where Jesus appears the blessed Trinity is understood as to my sight. ¶ And I said, "Benedicite, (ᛈᚻ) Dominus, (ᛋ) Domine, Blessed be the Lord." This I said for reverence in my meaning with a mighty voice, and full greatly was astonished for wonder and marvel that I had, that he who is so reverend and dreadful will be so homely with a sinful creature living in wretched flesh. ¶ This I took for the time of my temptation for I thought by the allowing of God, I should be tempted of fiends before I died. ¶ With this sight of the blessed Passion with the Godhead that I saw in my understanding I knew well that it was strength enough to me, Yea, and to all living creatures, against all the fiends of hell and ghostly temptation. ¶ In this he brought our blessed Lady to my understanding. I saw her ghostly in bodily likeness, a simple maiden and meek, young of age and little grown above a child, in the stature that she was when she conceived with child. (ᛒ) {Our gracious and good Lord (ᛒSᛈᚼ) God showed in part the wisdom and the truth of (ᛒ) the soul of our blessed Lady Saint Mary (ᛒSᛈᚼ) wherein I understood the reverent beholding that she beheld her God and Maker, marveling with great reverence that he would be born of her who was a simple creature of his making. For this was her marveling, that he who was her maker would be born of her who (ᚼ) was a simple creature of his making. (ᛒSᛈᚼ) ¶ And this wisdom and truth, knowing the greatness of his Maker and the littleness of her self, who is made, caused her to say full meekly to Gabriel, "Behold me, God's handmaiden." ¶ In this sight I understood truly that she is more than all that God made beneath her in worthiness and grace. For above her is nothing that is made but the blessed Christ as to my sight. (ᛒ) And this our good Lord showed to my understanding in teaching of us.

(S) How God is to us everything that is good, tenderly wrapping us. And all thing that is made, in regard to Almighty God it is nothing. And how man has no rest until ▨▨ he noughts himself and all thing for the love of God. (Sᛈ) The Fifth Chapter.

I n this same time, our Lord showed to me a ghostly sight of his homely loving. I saw that he is to us everything that is good and comfortable for us. ¶ He is our clothing that for love, wraps us, embraces us, and all becloses us, for tender love that he may never leave us, being to us all thing that is good as to my understanding. ¶ Also in this he showed a little thing the quantity of a hazelnut in the palm of my hand, and it was as round as a ball. I looked thereupon with the eye of my understanding and thought, "What may this be?" And it was generally answered thus, ¶ "It is all that is made." I marveled how it might last, for I thought it might suddenly have fallen to nought for littleness. ¶ And I was answered in my understanding, "It lasts and ever shall, for God loves it." And so all things have their being by the love of God. ¶ In this little thing I saw three properties: ¶ The first is that God made it; ¶ The second that God loves it; ¶ The third that God keeps it. ¶ But what is this to me, truly, the Maker, the Keeper, and the Lover, I cannot tell. For, till I am substantially oned to him I may never have full rest, nor true bliss; that is to say until I be so fastened to him, that there be right nought that is made between my God and me. (𝖂𝖕) This little thing that is made, I thought, might have fallen to nought for littleness. (𝕳) And who shall do this deed? Truly himself by his mercy and his grace, for he has made me for this and blissfully restored me thereto. In this blessed Revelation God showed me three noughts, of which noughts this is the first that was showed to me. ¶ Of this (𝕳) each man and woman who desires to live contemplatively needs to have knowledge (𝕊) of the littleness of creatures and (𝖂𝕤𝖕𝕳) to like as nought all things that are made, for to love and have God who is unmade. ¶ For this is the cause why we be not all in ease of heart and soul, for we (𝕳) who are occupied wilfully in earthly business and evermore seek worldly weal are not heirs of his in heart and in soul for to love and (𝖂𝕤𝖕𝕳) seek here rest, in these things that are so little wherein is no rest, and know not our God who is all mighty, all wise, all good. For he is the very rest. God will be known and he likes us to rest in him, for all that is beneath him does not suffice us. And this is the cause why no soul is rested, until it is noughted of all things that are made. When he is wilfully noughted for love to have him who is all, then is he able to receive ghostly rest. ¶ Also our Lord God showed that it is very great pleasure to him, that an innocent soul come ▨ to him nakedly, plainly, and homely. For this is the natural yearning of the soul by the touching of the holy Ghost, as by the understanding that I have in this Showing. "God, of your goodness give me yourself, for you are enough to me. And I may ask nothing that is less, that may be full worship to you. And if I ask anything that is less, ever I am in want, but only in you I have all." ¶ And these words are fully loving to the soul and very near touching the will of God and his goodness. For his goodness comprehends all his creatures and all his blessed works and overpasses without end. ¶ For he is the endlessness, and he has made us only to himself and restored us by his blessed Passion, and keeps us in his blessed love; and all this is of his goodness.

8

(S) How we should pray of the great tender love that our Lord has to man's soul, willing us to be occupied in knowing and loving of him. (Sp) The Sixth Chapter. (ꟿSp)

This Showing was made, to my understanding to teach our soul wisely to cleave to the goodness of God. And in that time the custom of our praying was brought to mind, how we use, for lack of understanding and unknowing of love to make many means. Then I saw truly that it is more worship to God, and more true delight that we faithfully pray to himself of his goodness, and cleave thereto by his grace with true understanding and steadfast belief, than if we made all the means that heart can think. ¶ For if we make all these means it is too little and not full worship to God. But in his goodness is all the whole, and there truly nought fails. ¶ For thus as I shall say came to my mind, in the same time, we pray to God for his holy flesh and for his precious blood, his holy Passion, his dearworthy death and wounds, and all the blessed nature, the endless life that we have of all this, is his goodness. ¶ And we pray him for his sweet mother's love, who bare him, and all the help we have of her, is of his goodness; And we pray for his holy Cross that he died on and all the virtue and the help that we have of the Cross, it is of his goodness. ¶ And in the same way all the help that we have of special ꟿ saints, and all the blessed company of heaven, the dearworthy love and endless friendship that we have of them, it is of his goodness. ¶ For God of his goodness, has ordained means to help us wholely fair and many. ¶ Of which the chief and principal means is the blessed nature that he took of the Maiden, with all the means that went before and come after, which belong to our redemption, and to endless salvation. ¶ Wherefore it pleases him that we seek him, and worship by means, understanding and knowing that he is the goodness of all. ¶ For the goodness of God is the highest prayer, and it comes down to the lowest part of our need. It quickens our soul and brings it to life and makes it to grow in grace and virtue. It is nearest in nature and readiest in grace. ¶ For it is the same grace that the soul seeks and ever shall till we know truly, who has us all in himself beclosed. ¶ (ꟿp) A man goes upright and the soul of his body is stored as in a full fair purse. And when it is time of his need, it is opened and shut again full honestly. ¶ And that it is he who does this, is showed there where he says that he comes down to us to the lowest part of our need. (ⓌⓈⓅ) For he has no contempt of what he has made, nor has he any disdain to serve us at the simplest office that belongs naturally to our body, for love of the soul, that he has made to his own likeness. ¶ For as the body is clothed in cloth, and the flesh in skin, and the bones in flesh, and the heart in the chest, so are we soul and body clad in the goodness of God and enclosed, Yea, and more homely. For all these may waste and wear away. The goodness of God is ever whole and nearer to us without any likeness. ¶ For truly our lover desires that our soul cleave to him with all our might and that we be ever more cleaving to his goodness. For of all things that our heart may think it pleases God most and soonest helps. ¶ For our soul is so specially loved of him who is highest, that it overpasses the knowing of all creatures ▨▨ ¶ That is to say there is no creature who is made who may understand how much and how sweetly, and how tenderly our Maker loves us, and therefore we may with his grace and his help stand in ghostly beholding with everlasting marveling in this high overpassing unmeasurable love, that almighty God has to us of his goodness. ¶ And therefore we may ask of our lover with reverence all that we will. For our natural will is to have God and the good will of God is to have us, and we may never cease of willing nor of longing till we have him in fullness of joy. ¶ And then may we no more will, for he will that we be occupied in knowing and loving till the time that we shall be fulfilled in heaven. ¶ And therefore was this lesson of love showed, with all that follows, as you shall see. For the strength and the ground of all was showed in the First Sight. For of all things the beholding and the loving of the Maker, makes the soul to seem least in his own sight and most fills it with reverent dread and true meekness, with plenty of charity to his even-Christian.

(Ⓢ) How our Lady beholding the greatness of her Maker thought herself least, and of the great drops of blood running from under the garland. And how the most joy to man is that God most high and mighty is holiest and most courteous. (ⓈⓅ) The Seventh Chapter.

And to teach us this as to my understanding our Lord God showed our Lady Saint Mary in the same time. That is to mean the high wisdom and truth she had in beholding of her Maker. (ⓌⓅ) This

10

wisdom and truth made her to behold her God, (⟨ⅢSⅮ⟩) so great, so high, so mighty, and so good. This greatness and this nobleness of the beholding of God fulfilled her of reverent dread, and with this she saw herself, so little and so low, so simple and so poor in regard of her Lord God, that this reverent dread fulfilled her of meekness. ⟨⟩ And thus by this ground she was fulfilled of grace and of all manner virtues and overpasses all creatures. ¶ In all the time that he showed this, that I have said, now in ghostly sight, I saw the bodily sight lasting of the plenteous bleeding of the head. The great drops of blood fell down from under the garland, seeming like pellets, as it had come out of the veins. And in the coming out it was brown red, for the blood was very thick. And in the spreading about it was bright red. And when it came to the brows, then it vanished. ¶ And notwithstanding the bleeding continued till many things were seen and understood. The fairness and the liveliness is like nothing but the same. ¶ The plenteousness is like to the drops of water that fall off the eaves of a house after a great shower of rain that fall so thick that no man may number them with bodily knowledge. And for the roundness it was like to the scale of herring, in the spreading on the forehead. ¶ These three came to my mind in that time, pellets for roundness in the coming out of the blood, the scale of herring in the spreading on the forehead for roundness, and raindrops from eaves for the innumerable plenteousness. ¶ This Showing was quick and lively and hideous and dreadful, sweet and lovely. And of all the sight it was most comfort to me that our God and Lord, who is so reverent and dreadful, is so homely and courteous. And this most fulfilled me with liking and secureness of soul. ¶ And to the understanding of this he showed this open example. It is the most honour that a solemn King or a great Lord may do to a poor servant, if he will be homely with him, and namely if he shows it himself, of a full true meaning and with a glad cheer both privately and openly. ⟨⟩ Then thinks this poor creature thus, "Ah, how might this noble Lord do more worship and joy to me than to show me, who am so simple this marvelous homeliness. Truly it is more joy and liking to me, than if he gave me great gifts and were himself aloof in manner." ¶ This bodily example was showed so high, that man's heart might be ravished and almost forget himself for joy of this great homeliness. Thus it fares by our Lord Jesus and by us. For truly it is the most joy that may be, as to my sight, that he who is highest and mightiest, noblest and worthiest, is lowest and meekest, homeliest and most courteous. And truly and surely this marvelous joy shall be shown us all when we see him. ¶

And this wills our Lord, that we will and trust, joy and delight, comforting us and solacing us, as we may with his grace and with his help,
into the time that we see it truly. For the most fullness of joy that we
shall have, as to my sight, is the marvelous courtesy and homeliness of
our Father who is our Maker in our Lord Jesus Christ, who is our
Brother and our Saviour. ¶ But this marvelous homeliness may no man
know in this time of life, but if he have it of special Showing of our
Lord, or of great plenty of grace inwardly given of the holy Ghost. But
faith and belief with charity deserve the reward, and so it is had by
grace. For in faith with hope and charity our life is grounded. The
Showing was made to whom God will plainly teach the same, opened
and declared with many secret points belonging to our faith which be
worshipful to know. ¶ And when the Showing which is given in a time
is passed and hid, then the faith keeps it by grace of the holy Ghost into
our life's end. ¶And thus by the Showing it is none other than the faith,
not less nor more, as it may be seen by our Lord's meaning in the same
matter by which it comes to the end.

13

(S) A recapitulation of what is said and how it was showed to her
generally for all. (SP) The Eighth Chapter. (SPA)

{A}nd as long as I saw this sight of the plenteous bleeding of the
head I might never cease of these words, "Benedicite Dominus,
Blessed be the Lord." In which Showing I understood six things. ¶ The
first is the tokens of the blessed Passion and the plenteous shedding
of his precious blood. ¶ The second is the Maiden who is dearworthy
Mother. ¶ The third is the blessedful Godhead who ever was, is and
ever shall be, all Mighty, all Wisdom, all Love. ¶ The fourth is all things
that he has made. For well I know that heaven and earth and all that is
made, is great and large, fair and good. But the cause why it showed so
little to my sight was because I saw it in the presence of him who is the
Maker of all things. For a soul who sees the maker of all, all that is made
seems fully little. ¶ The fifth is he who made all things for love, by the
same love it is kept and shall be without end. ¶ The sixth is that God is
every thing that is good as to my sight, and the goodness that all things
have, it is he. And all these our Lord showed me in the First Sight with

time and space to behold it. And the bodily sight ceased, and the ghostly sight dwelled in my understanding. And I stayed with reverent dread joying in what I saw. And I desired, as I dared, to see more, if it were his will, or else the same a longer time. ¶ In all this I was much stirred in charity to my even-Christian, that they might see and know the same that I saw. For I would it were comfort to them, for all. For this sight was showed in general, (Ⱶ) and nothing in particular. Of all that I saw this was the most comfort to me that our Lord is so homely and so courteous. And this most filled me with delight and secureness in soul. (SⱣⱵ) Then said I to them who were about me, "It is Doomsday today with me." And this I said for I believed I was dying. For that day when a man or woman dies, he is judged as he shall be without end, as to my understanding. ¶ This I said for I would they loved God the better, (Ⱶ) and set the less price by the vanity of the world, (SⱣⱵ) for to make them to have mind that this life is short as they might see in this example (Ⱶ) by me. (SⱣⱵ) For in all this time I thought to have died, and that was marvel to me and grief in part, for I thought this Vision was shown for them who should live. (Ⱶ)

{Ⱶ}ll that I saw (SⱣⱵ) of me, I mean in the person of all my even-Christians. For I am taught in the ghostly Showing of our Lord God that he means so. ¶ And therefore I pray you all for God's sake, and counsel you for your own profit that you leave the beholding of (Ⱶ) the wretched worldly sinful creature to whom it was showed, and mightily, wisely, and meekly behold God, who of his courteous love and endless goodness would show it generally in comfort of us all. And you who hear and see this vision and this teaching, that is of Jesus Christ to the edification of your soul. For it is God's will and my desire that you take it with great joy and liking, as Jesus had showed it unto you all as he did to me.

(S) Of the meekness of this woman keeping herself always in the faith of holy Church and how he who loves his even-Christian for God loves all things. (SⱣ) The Ninth Chapter. (SⱣⱵ)

ƒor the Showing I am not good but if I love God the better. (Ⱶ) And so may and so should every man do who sees it and hears it with good will and true meaning. And so is my desire that it should be to

every man the same profit that I desired to myself, and thereto was stirred by God the first time I saw it, for the common and general profit, as we are all one. And I am secure I saw it for the profit of many others. (SP) And inasmuch as you love God the better it is more to you than to me. ¶ I say not this to them who be wise, for they know it well, but I say it to you who be simple, for ease and comfort. For we are all one in comfort. For truly it was not showed me that God loved me better than the least soul who is in grace. For I am sure that there be many who never had Showing nor Sight but of the common teaching of holy Church, who love God better than I. For if I look singularly to myself, I am right nought. But in general I am, I hope, in oneness of charity with all my even-Christians. For in this onehead stands the life of all mankind that shall be saved. For God is all who is good unto my sight. (H) And if any man or woman sets aside his love from any of his even-Christians he truly loves right nought for he loves not all and so at that time he is not saved, for he is not in peace. (SPH) ¶ And God has made all that is made, and God loves all that he has made. And he who generally loves all his even-Christians for God, he loves all that is. For in mankind who shall be saved, is comprehended all, that is to say all that is made, and the Maker of all. For in man is God, and God is in all (H) and so in man is all. (S) And thus I desire love, and thus I love and thus I am saved. For I mean in the person of my even-Christian. And the more I love of this loving while I am here, the more I am like to the bliss that I shall have in heaven without end, who is God who of his endless love would become our brother and suffer for us. And I am secure, ¶ And I hope, by the grace of God, he who beholds it thus shall be truly taught and mightily comforted if he needs comfort. ⬛ (H)
But God forbid that you should say or take it so that I am a teacher, for I do not mean so. No, I never meant so. For I am a woman, unlearned, feeble, and frail. But I know well this that I say, I have it of the Showing of him who is sovereign teacher. But truly charity stirs me to tell you it. For I would God were known and my even-Christians helped, as I would be myself, to the more hating of sin and loving of God. But because I am a woman, should I therefore believe that I should not tell you the goodness of God? Since I saw in that same time that it is his will that it be known, and that you shall see well in the same matter that follows after, if it be well and truly taken. Then shall you soon forget me who am a wretch, and do what I do not stop, and behold Jesus who is the teacher of all. (SPH) I speak of them who shall be saved. For in this time God showed me none other. ¶ But in all things

I believe as holy Church believes, preaches, and teaches, for the faith of holy Church, which I had understanding beforehand and, as I hope by the grace of God, wilfully kept in use and custom, stood continually in my sight, willing and meaning never to receive anything that might be contrary thereunto. And with this intent I beheld the Showing with all my diligence. For in all this blessed Showing I beheld it as one in God's meaning, (Ħ) sight and I understand nothing in it that scandalizes or blocks me from the true teaching of holy Church. (SƿĦ)

{Ħll this (Ħ) blessed teaching of our Lord God (SƿĦ) was showed (Ħ) to me in three parts (SƿĦ) by threes, that is to say: by bodily sight; and by word formed in my understanding; and by ghostly sight. But the ghostly sight I cannot nor may not show it as openly nor as fully as I would. But I trust in our Lord God Almighty, that he shall, of his goodness, and for your love, make you to take it more ghostly and more sweetly than I can or may tell it. (Sƿ)

The Second Revelation (S) is of his discolouring, etc., and of our redemption and the discolouring of the Vernicle, and how it pleases God we seek him busily, abiding him steadfastly and trusting him mightily. (Sƿ) The Tenth Chapter. (SƿĦ)

{Ħnd after this I saw with bodily sight in the face of the Crucifix that hung before me, in the which I beheld continually a part of his Passion: contempt; spitting; and swallowing; and buffeting; and many langouring pains, more than I can tell; and often changing of colour. And one time I saw how half the face, beginning at the ear was covered over with (Ħ) all his blessed face at times closed in (SƿĦ) dry blood until it be closed to the mid-face. And after that the other half was closed in the same way. And there while it vanished in this part, even as it came. ¶ This I saw bodily, sorrowfully and darkly, and I desired more bodily sight to have seen more clearly. And I was answered in my reason, "If God will show you more he shall be your light. You need none but him." ¶ For I saw him be sought. For we are now so blind and so unwise that we never seek God, till he of his goodness shows himself to us. And when we see ought of him graciously, then are we stirred by the same grace to seek 🔲 with great desire to see him more blissfully. And thus I saw him and sought him, and I had him and I wanted him. And this is and should be our common working in this life as to my sight. One time my understanding was led down into the sea ground, and there I saw hills and dales seeming green as it were moss grown with wreck and with gravel. Then I understood thus, that if a man or woman were under the broad water, if he might have sight of God, so as God is with a man continually, he should be safe in body and soul, and take no harm. And overpassing, he should have more solace and comfort than all this world can tell. ¶ For he will that we believe that we see him continually though we think that it be but little. And in this belief he makes us evermore to get grace. For he will be seen, and he will be sought, he will be waited for, and he will be trusted. ¶ This Second Showing was so low, and so little, and so simple, that my spirits were in great travail, in the beholding, mourning, dreadful and longing, for I was sometimes in doubt whether it was a Showing or none. And then diverse times our good Lord gave me more sight, whereby I understood truly that it was a Showing. ¶ It was a figure and likeness of our foul dead skin, that our fair bright, blessed Lord bare for our sins. It made me to think of the holy Vernicle of Rome which he has portrayed with his own blessed face, when he was in his hard Passion, wilfully going to his death, and often changing of colour. Of the brownness and blackness, sadness and leanness. ¶ Of this image many marvel how it might be. Understanding that he portrayed it with his blessed face, which is the fairness of heaven, flower of earth, and the fruit of the Maiden's womb. Then how might this image be so discolouring and so far from fair? ¶ I desire to say as I have understood by the grace of God. ¶ We know in our faith, ▨▨▨ and believe by the teaching and preaching of holy Church, that the blessed Trinity made mankind to his image and to his likeness. In the same way we know that when man fell so deep, and so wretchedly by sin, there was no other help to restore man, but through him who made man. ¶ And he who made man for love, by the same love he would restore man to this same bliss, and overpassing. ¶ And like as we were like made to the Trinity in our first making, our Maker would that we should be like Jesus Christ our Saviour in Heaven without end, by the virtue of our again making. ¶ Then between these two he would for love and worship of man make himself as like to man in this deadly life in our foulness and our wretchedness, as man might be without guilt. Whereof it means, as it was said before, it was the image and likeness of our foul black dead skin, wherein our fair bright blessed Lord God is hid. ¶ But full surely I dare say and we ought to

17

trust that, so fair a man was never none but he, till what time his fair colour was changed, with travail and sorrow, and Passion dying. ¶ Of this it is spoken in the Eighth Revelation, where it treats more of the same likeness. And there it says of the Vernicle of Rome, it moves by diverse changing of colour and cheer, sometimes more comfortably and lively, and sometimes more ruthfully and deadly, as it may be seen in the Eighth Revelation. And this Vision was a learning to my understanding that the continual seeking of the soul pleases God very much, for it may do no more than seek, suffer, and trust. ¶ And this is wrought in the soul who has it by the holy Ghost. ¶ And the clearness of finding is of his special grace, when it is his will. The seeking with faith, hope, and charity pleases our Lord. And the finding pleases the soul and fulfills it with joy. ¶ And thus was I taught to my understanding, that seeking is as good as beholding, for the time that he will suffer the soul to be in travail. 🜔 It is God's will that we seek him to the beholding of him. For by that he shall show us himself of his special grace when he will. ¶ And how a soul shall have him in his beholding he shall teach himself, and that is most worship to him, and profit to yourself, and most receives of meekness and virtues with the grace and leading of the holy Ghost. For a soul that only fastens him on to God with true trust, either by seeking or in beholding, it is the most worship that he may do to him, as to my sight. ¶ These are two workings that must be seen in this Vision. That one is seeking. The other is seeing. The seeking is common that every soul has with his grace, and ought to have with discretion and teaching of the holy Church. It is God's will that we have three things in our seeking. ¶ The first is that we seek wilfully and busily without sloth, as it may be through his grace, gladly and merrily, without unreasonable heaviness and vain sorrow. ¶ The second is that we await him steadfastly for his love without grouching and striving against him at our life's end, for it shall last but a while. ¶ The third is that we trust in him mightily of full secured faith. For it is his will that we know he shall appear suddenly and blissfully to all his lovers. ¶ For his working is secret, and he will be perceived and his appearing shall be swift sudden, and he will be believed for he is most merciful and homely, Blessed must he be. (Sp)

18

The Third Showing. (S) How God does all things except sin, never changing his purpose without end. For he has made all things in fullness of
goodness. (SP) The Eleventh Chapter. (WSPH)

A nd after this I saw God in a point. That is to say in my understanding. By which sight I saw that he is in all things. I beheld attentively seeing and knowing in that sight that he does all that is done.
I marveled in that sight with a soft dread and thought "What is sin?"
For 🜨 I saw truly that God does all things, be it never so little. ¶
And I saw truly that nothing is done by chance, nor by luck, but all
things by the foreseeing wisdom of God. If it seem chance or fortune in
the sight of man, our blindness and our lack of foresight is the cause.
For the things that are in the foreseeing wisdom of God from without
beginning (which rightfully and worshipfully and continually he leads
to the best end as they come about), fall to us suddenly, ourselves un-
aware, and thus by our blindness and our lack of foresight we say they
are by chance or peradventure but to our Lord God they be not so.
Thus I understood in this Showing of Love. For well I know in the sight
of our Lord is no chance nor luck. But to our Lord God they be not so.
Wherefore I need to grant that all thing that is done, it is well done, for
our Lord God does all. For in this time the working of creatures was not
showed, but of our Lord God in the creature. For he is in the mid-point
of all things and all he does. ¶ And I was secure that he does no sin.
And here I saw truly that sin is no deed. (H) Therefore it seemed to me
that sin is nought. (SPH) For in all this sin was not showed. And I
would no longer marvel in this, but beheld our Lord what he would
show (H) me. (SP) ¶ And thus as it might be for the time being, the
rightfulness of God's working was showed to the soul. Rightfulness
has two fair properties. It is right and it is full. And so are all the works
of our Lord God. And thereto need neither the working of mercy and
grace. For it be all rightful, wherein nought fails. ¶ And in another time
he showed for the beholding of sin nakedly as I shall say. ¶ After where
he uses working of mercy and grace. And this Vision was showed to
my understanding. For our Lord will have the soul turned truly into
the beholding of him, and generally of all his works, for they are full
good. ¶ And all his doings be easy and sweet and bring the soul to
great ease, that is turned from the beholding of the blind judging of
man unto the fair sweet judging of our Lord God. ¶ For a man beholds
some 🜨 deeds well done and some deeds evil. But our Lord beholds
them not so. For as all that has being in nature is of God's making, so
are all things that are done in property of God's doing. For it is easy to

19

20

understand that the best deed is well done, and the highest, so well as the best deed is done, and the highest, so well is the least deed done, and all in property, and in the order that our Lord has ordained to it from without beginning. For there is no doer but he. (𝕎𝕊𝕡) ¶ I saw full surely that he never changes his purpose in any manner of thing nor ever shall without end. For there was nothing unknown to him in his rightful ordinance from without beginning. And therefore all things were set in order before anything was made. As it should stand without end. And no manner of thing shall fail of that point, for he made all things in fullness of goodness. ¶ And therefore the blessed Trinity is always most pleased in all his works. And all this he showed full blissfully. (𝕎) Also among other Showings, our good Lord, (𝕎𝕊𝕡) meaning thus, "See I am God. See I am in all things. See I do all things. See I never lift my hands from off my work, nor ever shall without end. See I lead all things to the end I ordained them to, and from without beginning, by the same might, wisdom, and love that I made them. How should anything be amiss?" ¶ Thus mightily, wisely and lovingly was the soul examined in this Vision. ¶ Then I saw truly that I needed to assent with great reverence, enjoying in God. (𝕊𝕡)

The Fourth Revelation. (𝕊) How God likes rather and better to wash us in his blood from sin than in water. For his blood is most precious. (𝕊𝕡) The Twelfth Chapter. (𝕊𝕡𝔸)

And after this I saw beholding the body plenteously bleeding (𝔸) hot and freshly and lively, right as I saw before in the head. And this was showed (𝕊𝕡𝔸) in the gashes from the scourging as thus. ¶ The fair skin was broken full deep into the tender flesh with sharp blows all about the sweet body so plenteously that where the hot blood ran out there was neither seen skin nor wound but as it were all blood. And when it came where it should have fallen down, then ⬛ it vanished, notwithstanding the bleeding continued a while till it might be seen with concern, and this was so plenteous to my sight that I thought, if it had been so in nature and in substance for that time, it should have made the bed all bloody and spilled over about. ¶ And then came to my mind that God has made waters plenteous on earth to our service, and to our bodily ease, for tender love that he has to us. But yet he likes better that we take most homely his blessed blood to wash us of sin. For there is no liquor that is made, that he likes so well to give us. For it is most plenteous, as it is most precious, and that by the virtue of his blessed Godhead. And it is our nature and all blessedly flows to us by the virtue of his precious love. ¶ The dearworthy blood of our Lord Jesus Christ, as truly as it is most precious, so truly is it most plenteous. ¶ Behold and see how the precious plenty of his dearworthy blood descended down into Hell and broke their bonds and delivered all that were there who belonged to the court of Heaven. ¶ The precious plenty of his dearworthy blood overflows all earth and is ready to wash all creatures of sin, who be of good will, have been and shall be. ¶ The precious plenty of his dearworthy blood ascends up into Heaven to the blessed body of our Lord Jesus Christ. And there is in him bleeding, and praying for us to the Father, and is, and shall be, as long as it needs. And evermore it flows in all heavens enjoying the salvation of all mankind, and that are there and shall be, fulfilling the number that fails.

⁂

The Fifth Revelation (S) is that the temptation of the fiend is overcome by the Passion of Christ to the increase of our joy and to his pain everlastingly. (Sp) The Thirteenth Chapter. (SpA)

And after, before God showed (A) to me (SpA) any words, he allowed me to behold in him a knowable time, and all that I had seen and all intellect, that was therein, as the simplicity of the soul might take it. ¶ Then he without voice and opening of lips, forms in my soul these words, "Herewith is the fiend overcome." These words our Lord said, meaning his blessed Passion as he showed (A) me (SpA) before. ¶ In this our Lord (A) brought into my mind and showed me (SpA) a part of the fiend's malice, and fully his weakness, for he showed that the Passion of him is the overcoming of the fiend. God showed (A) me (SpA) that the fiend has now the same malice that he had before the Incarnation. And as sore he travails and as continually he sees that all souls sent of salvation escape from him worshipfully by the virtue of Christ's precious Passion. And that is his sorrow and full evil he is humbled. ¶ For all that God allows him to do, turns us to joy, and him to shame and woe. And he has as much sorrow when God gives him leave to work as when he works not. And that is for he may never do as evil as he would. For his might is all taken in God's hands. But in God may be no wrath, as to my sight. ¶ For our Lord God endlessly has regard to his own worship. And to the profit of all who shall be saved. And with might and right he withstands the reproved, who of malice and shrewdness busy themselves to contrive and to do against God's will. ¶ Also I saw our Lord scorn his malice, and nought his weakness, and he will that we do so. For this sight I laughed mightily. And that made them to laugh, who were about me, and their laughing was a delight to me. I thought I would that all my even-Christians had been as I saw and then should they all laugh with me. But I saw not Christ laughing. But well I know that sight that he showed me, made me laugh. For I understood that we may laugh in comforting of ourselves, and joying in God. For the devil is overcome. ¶ And then I saw him scorn his malice. It was by leading of my understanding into our Lord. That is to say, an inward showing of truthfulness without changing of cheer. For as to my sight it is a worshipful property that is in God which is durable. ¶ And after this I fell into a sadness and said "I see three things, game, scorn and earnest. ¶ I see game that the fiend is overcome, I see scorn that God scorns him and he shall be scorned, and I see earnest that he is overcome by the blessed Passion and death of our Lord Jesus Christ, that was done in full earnest and with sad travail. ¶ And I said he is scorned. I mean that God scorns him, that is to say, for he sees him now, as he shall do without end. ¶ For in this God showed that the fiend is damned. And this I meant where I said, 'He shall be scorned,' at Doomsday generally of all who shall be saved to whose consolation he has great envy. For then he shall see that all the woe and tribulation that he has done to them shall be turned to the increase of their joy without end. And all the pain and tribulation that he would have brought them to shall endlessly go with him to Hell."

23

The Sixth Showing (**S**) is of the worshipful thanks with which he rewards his servants and it has three joys. (**SP**) The Fourteenth Chapter. (**SPH**)

After this our good Lord said, "I thank you for your work and namely of your youth." ¶ And in this my understanding was lifted up into Heaven, where I saw our Lord as a Lord in his own house who has

called all his dearworthy servants and friends to a solemn feast. Then
I saw the lord take no place in his own house. But I saw him royally
reign in his house and fulfill it with joy and mirth, himself endlessly to
gladden and to solace his dearworthy friends, full homely and full
courteously, with marvelous melody of endless love in his own fair
blessed cheer, which glorious cheer of the Godhead fulfills all Heavens
of joy and bliss. ¶

{G od showed (Ħ) me (ꟗꝓĦ) three degrees of bliss that every
soul shall have in heaven who willingfully has served God in
any degree on earth. ¶ The first is the worshipful thanks of our Lord
God, that he shall receive when he is delivered of pain. This thanking is
so high and so worshipful that he thinks it fills him, though there were
no more bliss. For I thought that all the pain and travail that might be
suffered of all living men might not deserve the worshipful thanks, that
one man shall have who wilfully has served God. ¶ The second is
that all the blessed creatures that are in Heaven shall see that worshipful thanking of our Lord God. And he makes his service known to all
who are in Heaven. And in this time this example was showed. A King,
if he thanks his servants, it is a great honour to them, and if he makes it
known to all the realm then is his worship much increased. The third is
that as new, and as pleasing as it is received at that time, right so shall it
last without end. And I saw that homely and sweetly was this said and
showed (Ħ) to me, (ꟗꝓĦ) that the age of every man shall be known in
Heaven, and shall be rewarded for his willing service and for his time.
And namely the age of them who willingfully and freely offer their
youth to God, is passingly rewarded and wonderfully thanked. For
I saw that when or what time a man or woman be truly turned to God
for one day's service and for his endless will, he shall have all these
three degrees of bliss. And the more that the loving soul sees this courtesy
of God, the more willing he is to serve him all his life.

⁂

(ꟗ) The Seventh Revelation is of often feeling weal and woe, etc. And
how it is expedient that man sometimes be left without comfort, it not
causing sin. (ꟗꝓ) The Fifteenth Chapter. (ꟗꝓĦ)

A nd after this he showed a sovereign ghostly liking in my soul. I
was fulfilled of the everlasting secureness, mightily sustained

without any painful dread. ¶ This feeling was so glad and so ghostly that I was all in peace, and in rest, so that there was nothing in earth that should have grieved me. This lasted but a while, and I was turned and left to my self in heaviness, and weariness of my life, and disgust of myself, that scarcely I could have the patience to live. There was no comfort, nor any ease for me, but faith, hope, and charity. And these I had in truth, but little in feeling. ¶ And soon after this our blessed Lord gave me again the comfort and the rest in soul in liking and secureness so blissful and so mighty, that no dread nor sorrow, nor bodily pain that might be ▨▨▨ suffered, should have diseased me. And then the pain showed again to my feeling. And then the joy and the liking. And now that one and now that other, diverse times. I suppose about twenty times. And in the same time of joy, I might have said with Saint Paul, "Nothing shall separate me from the charity of Christ." And in the pain I might have said with Saint Peter, "Lord, save me. I perish." ¶ This vision was showed me after my understanding: that it is helpful to some souls to feel in this way. ¶ Sometimes to be in comfort, and sometimes to fail and to be left to himself. God wills that we know that he keeps us even alike, secure, in weal and in woe, (Ⱨ) and as much loves us in woe as in weal. (SƿⱧ) And for profit of man's soul, a man is sometimes left to himself, although sin is not ever the cause. For in this time I sinned not, wherefore should I be left to myself? For it was so sudden. ¶ Also, I deserved not to have this blessed feeling, but freely our Lord gives it when he will. And allows us to be in woe sometimes. And both is one love. ¶ For it is God's will, that we hold us in comfort with all our might. For bliss is lasting without end, and pain is passing and shall be brought to nought to them who shall be saved. ¶ And therefore it is not God's will that we follow the feeling of pain in sorrow and mourning for them, but suddenly passing over and holding us in endless bliss, that is God Almighty, our lover and keeper. (Sƿ)

The Eighth Revelation (S) is of the last piteous pains of Christ dying, and discolouring of his face and drying of his flesh. (Sƿ) The Sixteenth Chapter. (SƿⱧ)

{Ⱨ}fter this Christ showed a part of his Passion near his dying. I saw his sweet face as it was dry and bloodless with pale dying.

And since more pale dead langouring, and then turned more dead into blue, and since more blue, and the flesh turned more deeply dead. For his Passion showed for me most properly in his blessed face, and namely in his lips. There I saw these four colours. Those that were before fresh, ruddy, and pleasing to my sight ¶ This was a ghastly change to see this deep dying. And also the nose shriveled and dried to my sight. And the sweet body was brown and black, all turned out of fair lively colour of himself unto dry dying. For each time that our Lord and blessed Saviour died upon the Cross it was a dry, yowling wind and wonder cold as to my sight. And what time the precious blood was bled out of the sweet body that might pass there from, yet there dwelled a moisture in the sweet flesh of Christ as it was showed. ¶ Bloodlessness and pain, drying within and blowing of wind and cold coming from without, met together in the sweet body of Christ. And these four, two without and two within, dried the flesh of Christ by process of time. And though this pain was bitter and sharp yet it was full long lasting as to my sight. And painfully dried up all the lively spirits of Christ's flesh. Thus I saw the sweet flesh die in gashes, by part after part, drying with marvelous pains. And as long as any spirit had life in Christ's flesh, so long suffered he pain. ¶ This long pining seemed to me as if he had been seven nights dying to the point of passing away, suffering the last pain. And when I said it seemed to me as if he had been seven nights dead, it means that the sweet body was so discoloured, so dry, so shriveled, so deadly and so piteous as he had been seven nights dead, continually dying. ¶ And I thought the dying of Christ's flesh was the most pain and the last of his Passion.

(S) Of the grievous bodily thirst of Christ caused four ways and of his piteous crowning and of the most pain to a natural lover. (SP) The Seventeenth Chapter. (SPA)

And in this dying was brought to my mind the words of Christ, "I thirst." For I saw in Christ a double thirst, one bodily, another ghostly, which I shall speak of in the Thirty-First Chapter. And for the ghostly thirst was showed (A) to me, (SPA) for the bodily thirst, which I understood was caused from failing of moisture. For the blessed flesh and bones were left all alone without blood and moisture. The blessed body dried alone a long time, with wringing of the nails, (Ⴙ) weight of the head, and (SⲢႵ) weight of the body. For I understood that for tenderness of the sweet hands and of the sweet feet, by the largeness, hardness, and grievousness ▨▧▨ of the nails, the wounds waxed wide and the body sagged by the weight hanging a long time, and the piercing and wringing of the head and binding of the crown all baked with dry blood with the sweet hair clinging and the dry flesh to the thorns, and the thorns to the dying flesh. ¶ And in the beginning, while the flesh was fresh and bleeding the continual setting of the thorns made the wounds wide. And furthermore I saw that the sweet skin and the tender flesh with the hair and the blood were all raised and loosed above from the bone with the thorns and broken in many pieces from where it was dagged in many pieces as a cloth that was sagging. And were hanging as it would have fallen for heaviness and looseness while it had natural moisture. And that was great sorrow and dread to me. ¶ For I thought I would not for my life have seen it fall. How it was done I saw not. But understood it was with the sharp thorns and the boistrous and grievous setting on of the Garland unsparingly and without pity. This continued awhile and soon it began to change. And I beheld and marveled how it might be. And then I saw it was, for it began to dry, and ceased a part of the weight and set about the garland. And thus it environed all about, as it were, garland upon garland. The Garland of the Thorns was dyed with the blood and the other garland and the head was all one colour as clotted blood, when it is dry. The skin of the flesh that was gashed of the face and of the body was in small wrinkles with a tawny colour like a dry board when it is kilned. And the face more brown than the body. I saw four manner of dryings. ¶ The first was bloodless. ¶ The second was pain following after. ¶ And third is that he was hanging up in the air as men hang a cloth to dry. ¶ The fourth, that the bodily nature asks for liquid. And there was no manner comfort ministered to him in all his woe and disease. Ah, hard and grievous was his pain. But much harder and more grievous it was, when the moisture failed, and all began to dry, thus shriveling. These were the pains that showed in the blessed head. ¶ The first wrought ▨▧▨ to the dying while it was moist. ¶ And that other slow with clinging drying with blowing of the wind from without, that dried him more and pained with cold than my heart can think. And other pains, for which pains I saw that all is too little that I can say, for it may not be told. (Ⴙ) But each soul after the saying of Saint Paul should feel in him that in Christ Jesus. (SⲢႵ) The which Showing of Christ's pains filled me full of pain. For I knew well he suffered but once, but as he would show it to me and fill me with mind as I had before desired. (Ħ) My mother stood among the others and beholding me, lifted up her hand before my face to close my eyes. For she believed I was already dead or else that I had died, and this greatly increased my sorrow. For notwithstanding all my pains, I would not have been stopped for love that I had in him. (SpĦ) And in all this time of Christ's pains, I felt no pain, but for Christ's pains. Then I thought I knew but little what pain it was that I asked and as a wretch I repented, thinking if I had known what it had been I would be loath to have prayed it. ¶ For I thought it passed bodily death my pains. I thought, "Is any pain like this?" And I was answered in my reason, "Hell is another pain, for there is despair." (Ħ) "Despair is more, for that is ghostly pain. But bodily pain is not more than this." (Sp) But of all pains that lead to salvation, this is the most pain, to see your love suffer. ¶ How might any pain be more to me than to see him who is all my life, my bliss and all my joy, suffer. ¶ Here I felt truly that I loved Christ so much above my self, (Ħ) that I thought, it had been a great ease to me to have died bodily, (Sp) that there was no pain that might be suffered like to that sorrow that I had to see him in pain.

(S) Of the spiritual martyrdom of our Lady and other lovers of Christ. And how all things suffered him good and ill. (Sp) The Eighteenth Chapter. (SpĦ)

Here I saw a part of the compassion of our Lady Saint Mary, for Christ and she were so oned in love, that the greatness of his loving was cause of the greatness of her pain. For in this I saw a substance of natural love continued by grace that creatures have to him, which natural love was most fully showed in his sweet Mother and overpassing, for so much as she loved him more than all others, her pains passed all others. For ever the higher, the mightier, the sweeter that the love be the more sorrow it is to the lover to see that body in pain that is loved. ¶ And all his disciples and all his true lovers suffered pains more than their own bodily dying. For I am secure by my own feeling that the least of them loved him so far above themselves that it passes all that I can say. ¶ Here I saw a great oneing between Christ and us to my

29   understanding. For when he was in pain, we were in pain, and
all creatures who might suffer pain suffered with him. ¶ That is to say,
all creatures (Sℙ) that God has made to our service. The firmament,
the earth, failed for sorrow in their nature, in the time of Christ's dying.
For it belongs naturally to their property to know him for their God in
whom all their virtue stands. ¶ When he failed then they needed for
nature to fail with him as much as they might for sorrow of his pains.
And thus those who were his friends suffered pain for love. And generally all, that is to say, they who knew him not, suffered for failing of
all manner of comfort, save the mighty secret keeping of God. I mean
two kinds of folk, as it may be understood, by two persons, who knew
him not, that one was Pilate, that other was Saint Dionysius of France,
who was at that time a pagan. For when he saw wondrous and marvelous sorrows and dreads that befell in that time, he said, "Either the
world is now at an end or else he who is maker of nature suffers." ¶
Wherefore he did write on an altar, "This is the Altar of the Unknown
God." God of his goodness who makes the planets and the elements to
work in their nature to the blessed man, and the cursed. ¶ In that time
it was withdrawn from both, wherefore it was, that they who knew
him not were in sorrow that time. ¶ Thus was our Lord Jesus noughted
for us, and we stand all in this manner noughted with him, and shall
do till we come to his bliss as I shall say after.

(S) Of the comfortable beholding of the Crucifix, and how the desire of
the flesh without consent of the soul is no sin; and the flesh must be
in pain suffering until both be oned to Christ. (Sℙ) The Nineteenth
Chapter. (Sℙℍ)

In this I would have looked up from the Cross and I dared not, for I
knew well, while I beheld the Cross I was secure and safe; therefore
I would not assent to put my soul in peril. ¶ For beside the Cross was
no secureness but ugliness of fiends. Then a suggestion was made in
my reason, as if it was friendly said (ℙℍ) to me (Sℙℍ), "Look up to
heaven to his Father." And then I saw with the faith that I felt, that
there was nothing (ℍ) to me (Sℙℍ) between the Cross and heaven that
might have diseased me. ¶ Either I had to look up or else to answer. ¶
I answered inwardly with all the strength of my soul and said, "Nay,

I may not: for you are my heaven." This I said for I would not. For I had rather been in that pain till Doomsday, than come to heaven otherwise than by him. For I knew well that he who bound me so sore should unbind me when he would. ¶

Thus I was taught to choose Jesus to my heaven whom I saw only in pain at that time, I wanted no other heaven than Jesus, who shall be my bliss when I come there. And this has ever been a comfort to me, that I chose Jesus to be my heaven by his grace in all this time of Passion and sorrow. ¶ And that has been a learning to me that I should ever more do so, choosing only Jesus to my heaven, in weal and woe. And though I as a wretch had repented, as I said before if I had known what pain it had been, I would have been loath to have prayed. ¶ Here I saw truly that it was begrudging and damning of the flesh without assent of the soul, in which God assigns no blame. Repenting and wilful choice be two contraries, which I felt both at the one and the same time, and they be two parts, one outward, that other inward. ¶ The outward part is our deadly fleshliness which is now in pain and woe and shall be in this life. Whereof I felt much at this time, and that part was that repented. ¶ The inward part is a high blissful life, which is all in peace and in love. And this was more secretly felt. And this part is in which mightily, wisely and wilfully I chose Jesus to be my heaven. ¶ And in this I saw truly that the inward part is master and sovereign to the outward, and not charging nor paying heed to the will of that, but all the intent and will is set endlessly to be oned into our Lord Jesus. ¶ That the outward part should draw the inward to assent, was not showed to me, but that the inward draws the outward by grace, and both shall be oned in bliss without end by the virtue of Christ, this was showed.

30

(S) Of the unspeakable Passion of Christ and of three things of the Passion always to be remembered. (SP) The Twentieth Chapter. (SPH)

And thus I saw our Lord Jesus langouring a long time, for the oneing of the Godhead gave strength to the manhood, for love to suffer more than all man might suffer. I mean not only more pain than all men might suffer, but also that he suffered more pain than all men of salvation who ever were from the first beginning until the last day (H) no tongue might tell or heart fully think, the pains that our Saviour suffered for us, (SⱣⱧ) having regard to the worthiness of the highest worshipful king, and the shameful, despicable painful death. For he who is highest and worthiest was most fully noughted and utterliest despised. (Ⱨ) But the love that made him to suffer all this, it passes as much his pains as heaven is above earth. For the pains were deeds done in a time by the working of love. But love was without beginning and is and ever shall be without any end. (SⱣ) For the highest point that may be seen in the Passion is to think and know who he is who suffered. (Ᵽ) Seeing after these two other points which be lower. ¶ That one is what he suffered. ¶ And that other, for whom he suffered. (SⱣ) And in this he brought a part in mind the height and nobility of the glorious Godhead, and therewith the preciousness and the tenderness of the blissful body which be oned together. And also the loathing that is in our nature to suffer pain. For as much as he was most tender and clean, right so was the most strong and mighty to suffer. And for every one's sin who shall be saved he suffered, and every man's sorrow. And desolation he saw and sorrowed, for naturalness and love. For in as much as our Lady sorrowed for his pains, as much he suffered sorrow for her sorrow. And more, in as much as the sweet manhood of him was worthier in nature. For as long as he was mortal he suffered for us, and sorrowed for us. And now he is uprisen and no more deadly, yet he suffered with us. ¶ And I beholding all this by his grace, saw that the love of him was so strong which he has to our soul, that wilfully he chooses it with great desire. And mildly he suffered it with well paying. For the soul who beholds it thus, when it is touched by grace he shall truly see that the pains of Christ's Passion pass all pains, that is to say, which pains shall be turned into everlasting overpassing joys by the virtue of Christ's Passion.

31

(S) Of three beholdings in the Passion of Christ and how we be now dying in the Cross with Christ, but his cheer puts away all pain. The Twenty-First Chapter. (SⱣ)

It is God's will as to my understanding that we have three ways of beholding in his blessed Passion. The first is the hard pain that he suffered with contrition and compassion. And that showed our Lord in this time. And gave me might and grace to see it. ¶ And I looked after the departing with all my might and thought to have seen the body all dead, but I saw him not so. And right in the same time that I thought it seemed the life might no longer last and the showing of the end needs must be. (ρ)

Suddenly (I beholding in the same Cross), he changed his blissful cheer. The changing of his blissful cheer changed mine. And I was as glad and merry as it was possible to be. Then brought our Lord merrily to my mind, "Where is now any point of the pain or of your grief?" And I was full merry. I understood that we be now in our Lord's meaning in his Cross with him in our pains and our Passion dying, and we wilfully abiding in the same Cross with his help and his grace into the last point, suddenly he shall change his cheer to us, and we shall be with him in heaven. Between that one and that other shall be (S) no (ρ) one (Sρ) time. And then shall all be brought to joy. And so meant he in this Showing. "Where is now any point of your pain or your grief?" And we shall be fully blessed. ¶ And here I saw truly that if he showed us now his blissful cheer, there is no pain on earth or in any other place that should grieve us, but all things should be to us joy and bliss. But for he shows to us the time of Passion as he bore in this life and his Cross, therefore we are in disease and travail with him as our frailty asks. And the cause why he suffers is because he will for his goodness make us be the heir with him in his bliss. And for this little pain that we suffer here, we shall have a high endless knowing in God which we might never have without that. And the harder our pains have been with him in his Cross, the more shall our worship be with him in his kingdom.

32

Then said our good Lord Jesus Christ asking, "Are you well paid that I suffered for you?" I said, "Yea, good Lord, thanks, Yea, good Lord," "Blessed must you be." Then said Jesus our natural Lord, "If you are paid, I am paid, It is a joy, a bliss, an endless liking to me that ever I suffered Passion for you. And if I might suffer more I would have suffered more." In this feeling my understanding was lifted up into heaven. And there I saw three heavens, of which sight I greatly marveled. And thought, "I see three heavens and all the blessed manhood of Christ, none is more, none is less, none is higher, none is lower, but even like in bliss." ¶ For the first heaven Christ showed me his Father in no bodily likeness but in his property and in his working. That is to say I saw in Christ that the Father is. The working of the Father is this, that he gives reward to his Son Jesus Christ. This gift and this reward is so blissful to Jesus, that his Father might have given him no reward that might have delighted him better. ¶ For the first heaven that is the pleasing of the Father, showed to me as a heaven, and it was full blissful. For he is well pleased with all the deeds that Jesus has done about our salvation. Wherefore we be not only his by his buying, but also by the courteous gift of his Father. We be his bliss, we be his reward, we be his worship, we be his crown. And this was a singular marvel and a full delectable beholding, that we be his crown. This that I say is so great bliss to Jesus that he sets at nought all his travail and his hard Passion and his cruel and shameful death. And in these words, "If that I might suffer more I would suffer more," I saw truly that as often as he might die, so often he would (Ⱶ) die once for each man who shall be saved, as he died once for all, (ⱲSⱣႻ) and love should never let him have rest, till he had done it. ¶ And I beheld with great diligence to know how often he would die if he might. And truly the number passed my understanding and my wits so far, that my reason might not nor could comprehend it. And when he had thus often died or should, yet he would set it at nought for love. For all he thinks but little in regard of his love. For though the sweet manhood of Christ might suffer but once, the goodness in him may never cease being offered. Every day he is ready to the same if it might be. ¶ For if he said he would for my love make new heavens and new earth, it were but little in reward. For this might be done every day if he would, without any travail. ¶ But for to die for my love so often that the number passes natural ⚌ reason, it is the highest offer that our Lord God might make to man's soul as to my sight. Then means he thus, "How should it then be, that I should not for your love do all that I might, which deed grieves me not, since I would for your love die so often, having no reward for my hard pains." And here I saw for the second beholding in this blessed Passion, the love that made him to suffer passes as far all his pains, as heaven is above earth. For the pains was a noble, (Ᵽ) precious, and (SⱣ) worshipful deed done in a time by the working of love. And love was without beginning, is, and shall be without ending. For which love he said full sweetly (Ⅎ) And that he showed me well, saying (ＰＳℲ) these words, "If I might suffer more, (ＰＳ) I would suffer more." (ＳＰℲ) He said not, "If it were needful to suffer more," (ＰℲ) but, "If I might suffer more." (ＳＰℲ) For though it were not needful, but if he might suffer more he would. ¶ This deed and this work about our salvation was ordained as well as God might ordain it. (ＰℲ) It was done as worshipfully as Christ might do it. (ＳＰℲ) And here I saw a full bliss in Christ. For his bliss should not have been full, if it might have been done any better (ＰℲ) than it was done.

(Ｓ) How Christ will we joy with him greatly in our Redemption and to desire grace of him that we may do so. (ＳＰ) The Twenty-Third Chapter. (ＷＳＰℲ)

Ａnd in these three words, "It is a joy, a bliss, an endless liking to me," were showed (Ⅎ) to me (ＳＰℲ) three heavens. As thus, for the joy I understand the pleasure of the Father, and for the bliss, the worship of the Son, and for the endless liking, the holy Ghost. The Father is pleased, the Son is worshiped, the holy Ghost delights. ¶ And here I saw, for the third beholding, in his blissful Passion, that is to say, the joy and the bliss that make him like it. For our courteous Lord showed his Passion to me in five ways: ¶ Of which the First is the bleeding of the head. ¶ The Second is the discolouring of his face. ¶ The Third is the plenteous bleeding of the body from the gashes of the scourging. ¶ The Fourth is the deep dying. These four are aforesaid for the pains of the Passion. ¶ And the Fifth is that was showed for the joy and the bliss of the Passion. For it is God's will that we have true liking with him in our salvation. And therein he will we be mightily comforted and strengthened, and thus will he merrily with his grace that our soul be occupied. For we are his bliss. For in us he joys without end. And so shall we in him with his grace. And all that he has done for us and does and ever shall was never cost nor charge to him nor might be, but only that he died in our manhood, beginning at the sweet Incarnation and lasting till the blessed Uprising on Easter Morn. So long lasted the cost and the charge about our redemption in deed, of which deed he joys endlessly as it is before said. ¶ Jesus wills we take heed to the bliss that is in the blissful [image] Trinity of our salvation and that we desire to have as much ghostly liking with his grace as it is before said. That is to say that the liking of our salvation be like the joy that Christ has of our salvation, as it may be while we are here. All the Trinity wrought in the Passion of Christ, ministering abundance of virtues, and plenty of grace to us by him. But only the Maiden's Son suffered. Whereof all the blessed Trinity endlessly joys. And this was showed in these words, "Are you well paid?" And by that other word that Christ said, "If you are well paid then I am well paid." As if he said, "It is joy and liking enough to me. And I ask nought else of you for my travail but that I might well pay you." ¶ And in this he brought to mind the property of a glad Giver. Ever a glad Giver takes but little heed of the thing that he gives, but all his desire, and all his intent is to please him and solace him to whom he gives it. And if the receiver take the gift highly and thankfully, then the courteous Giver sets at nought all his cost and all his travail, for the joy and delight that he has. For he has pleased and solaced him whom he loves. Plenteously, and fully was this showed (Ⱶ) to me. (SⱣⱵ) Think also wisely of the greatness of this word, "That ever I suffered Passion for you." For in that was showed a high knowing of love and delight that he has in our salvation with manifold joys that follow of the Passion of Christ. ¶ One is that he joys that he has done it in deed. And he shall no more suffer. ¶ Another, that he brought us up into heaven and made us for to be his crown and endless bliss. Another is that he has therewith bought us from endless pains of Hell.

(Ᵽ) The Tenth Revelation (S) is that our Lord Jesus shows in love his blessed heart even cloven in two, enjoying. (SⱣ) The Twenty-Fourth Chapter.

With a glad cheer, (Ⱶ) **{f**ull merrily and gladly (ⱲSⱣⰝ) our Lord looked into his side, and beheld enjoying, and with his sweet looking he led forth the understanding of his creature by the same wound into his side within. And then he showed a fair delectable place and large enough for all mankind that shall be saved to rest in peace and in love. And therewith he brought to mind his dearworthy blood and precious water which he let pour all out for love. And with the sweet beholding he showed his blissful heart even cloven in two. And with this sweet enjoying he showed to my understanding in part the blessed Godhead stirring then the pure soul to understand, as it may be said. That is to mean the endless love, that was without beginning and is and shall be ever. ¶ And with this our good Lord said full blissfully, "Lo, how I love you." As if he had said, (ꟼ) "My child, if you cannot look in my Godhead, see here. How I let open my side, and my heart is cloven in two and lets out blood and water, all that is in it, and this delights me and so will it delight you." (ꟿsp) "My darling, behold and see your Lord your God who is your Maker and your endless joy. (ꟿp) See your own brother, your (ꟿ) Sovereign (p) Saviour, (ꟿp) my child, behold. (ꟿsp) See what liking and bliss I have in your salvation. And for my love joy now with me." ¶ And also for more understanding this blessed word was said, "Lo, how I love you." As if he had said, "Behold and see that I loved you so much before I died for you, that I would die for you, and now I have died for you and suffered willfully that I may. And now is all my bitter pain and all my hard travail turned to endless joy and bliss to me. And to you. How should it now be, that you should pray anything of me that delights me, but if I should full gladly grant it to you. For my delight is your holiness and your endless joy and bliss with me." This is the understanding simply as I can say of this blessed word, "Lo, how I loved you." (ꟿspꟼ) This showed our good Lord for to make us glad and merry. (sp)

35

The Eleventh Revelation (s) is a high ghostly showing of his Mother. (sp) The Twenty-Fifth Chapter. (spꟼ)

And with this same cheer of mirth and joy, our good Lord looked down on the right side. And brought to my mind where our Lady stood in the time of his Passion, and said, "Will you see her?" And in this sweet word as if he had said, "I know well you would see my blessed mother, for after myself she is the highest joy that I might show you and most pleasing and honour to me. And most she is desired to be seen of my blessed creatures." And for the high marvelous singular love that he has to this sweet Maiden, his blessed Mother, our Lady Saint Mary, he showed her highly enjoying, as by the meaning of these sweet words. As if he said, "Will you see how I love her, that you may joy with me in the love that I have in her and she in me?" ¶ And also to more understanding of this sweet word our Lord God speaks to all mankind who shall be saved. As it were all to one person as if he said, "Will you see in her how you are loved? For your love I made her so high, so noble, and so worthy, and this delights me. And so will I that it does you." For after himself she is the most blessed sight. But here I am not taught to long to see her bodily presence while I am here. But the virtues of her blessed soul, her truth, her wisdom, her charity, whereby I may learn to know myself and reverently dread my God. And when our good Lord had showed this, (Ⱨ) and with the same cheer and mirth he looked down on the right side and brought to my mind where our Lady stood in the time of the Passion (ＳＰⱧ) and said this word, "Will you see her?" I answered and said, "Yea, good Lord, thanks. Yea, good Lord, if it be your will." Often I prayed this and I thought I would have seen her in bodily presence, but I saw her not so, and Jesus in that word showed me a ghostly sight of her. Right as I had seen her before, little and simple, so he showed her then high and noble and glorious, and pleasing to him above all creatures. And he will that it be known that all those who delight in him should delight in her and in the delight that he has in her and she in him. And to more understanding he showed this example: As if a man love a creature singularly above all creatures, he will make all creatures to love and to like that creature whom he loves so much. And in this word that Jesus said, "Will you see her?" I thought it was the most delightful word that he might have given me of her with the ghostly Showing that he gave me of her. For our Lord showed me nothing in special, but our Lady Saint Mary and her he showed (Ⱨ) me (ＳＰⱧ) three times. ¶ The First was as she was pregnant. ¶ The Second was as she was in her sorrows under the Cross. ¶ The third is as she is now in delight, worship, and joy. (ＳＰ)

The Twelfth Revelation (Ｓ) is that the Lord our God is all sovereign being. (ＳＰ) The Twenty-Sixth Chapter. (ＳＰⱧⱲ)

Ⱨ nd after this our Lord showed him (Ⱨ) to me (ＳＰⱧⱲ) more glorified as to my sight, than I saw him before. Wherein I was taught that our soul shall never have rest till it comes to him knowing that he is fullness of joy, (Ⱶ) each contemplative soul to whom it is given to look for and to seek God shall see him, and pass into God by contemplation. And after this teaching, (ⱽ ⱷ Ⱶ Ⱚ) homely and courteously blissful and true life. Our Lord Jesus often times said "I it am, I it am, I it am, who is highest, I it am whom you love, I it am whom you like, I it am whom you serve, I it am whom you long for, I it am whom you desire, I it am whom you mean, I it am who is all, I it am whom holy Church preaches and teaches you, I it am who showed myself here to you." The number of the words passes my wit and all my understanding and all my might, and it is the highest as to my sight. For therein is comprehended I cannot tell, but the joy that I saw in the Showing of them passes all that the heart may will, and soul may desire. And therefore the words be not declared here, but every man, after the grace that God gives him in understanding and loving, receives them in our Lord's meaning.

The Thirteenth Revelation (ⱽ) is that our Lord God wills that we have great regard to all his deeds that he has done in the great nobleness of making all things, and how sin is not known but by the pain. (ⱽ ⱷ Ⱚ) The Twenty-Seventh Chapter. (ⱽ ⱷ Ⱶ Ⱚ)

After this the Lord brought to my mind the longing that I had to him before. And I saw that nothing hindered me but sin. And so I beheld generally in us all. And I thought if sin had not been, we should all have been clean and like to our Lord as he made us. And thus in my folly before this time, often I wondered why, by the great foreseeing wisdom of God, the beginning of sin was not stopped. For then thought I all should have been well. ¶ This stirring and thought in my mind I should have forsaken and not have yielded to it. ¶ And nevertheless I made mourning and sorrow therefore, without reason and discretion. But Jesus, who in this Vision informed me of all that I needed, (Ⱶ) I say not that I need more teaching, for our Lord, with the Showing of this, has left me to holy Church, and I am hungry and thirsty and needy and sinful and frail and wilfully submit myself to the teaching of holy Church with all my even-Christians to the end of my life. He (ⱽ ⱷ) answered in this word and said, "Sin is needful, but all shall be well. And all shall be well. And all manner of thing shall be well." In this

naked word, "Sin," our Lord brought to my mind generally all
that is not good. And the shameful despite and the utter noughting that
he bare for us, in this life, and his dying and all the pains and passions
of all his creatures, ghostly and bodily. For we be all in part noughted
and we shall be noughted following our Master Jesus, till we be fully
purged, that is to say, till we be fully noughted of our (Ħ) own (SρĦ)
deadly flesh, and of all our inward affections, which are not very good.
¶ And the beholding of this with all pains that ever were or ever shall
be. And with all these I understand the Passion of Christ, for the most
pain. And overpassing. And all this was showed (Ħ) me (SρĦ) in a
touch, and readily passed over into comfort. ¶ For our good Lord would
not that the soul were afraid of this ugly sight. But I saw not sin. For I
believe it has no manner of substance nor any part of being, nor might
it be known but by the pain that it causes. And this pain, it is something
as to my sight for a time. For it purges and makes us to know ourself
and ask mercy. For the Passion of our Lord is comfort to us against all
this. And so is his blessed will. And for the tender love that our good
Lord has to all who shall be saved, he comforts readily and sweetly,
meaning thus, "It is true that sin is the cause of all this pain, but all shall
be well, and all shall be well, and all manner of thing shall be well." ¶
These words were said full tenderly, showing no manner of blame to
me nor to none who shall be saved. Then were it a great unnaturalness
(ρĦ) of me (SρĦ) to blame or wonder on God for my sin, since he
blames not me for sin. ¶ And in these same words I saw a marvelous
high secret hid in God, which privity he shall openly make known to
us in heaven. ¶ In which knowing we shall truly see the cause why
he suffered sin to come. In which sight we shall endlessly joy in our
Lord God.

<hr />

How the Children of Salvation shall be shaken in sorrows, but Christ
enjoys with compassion, and a remedy against tribulation. (Sρᛁ) The
Twenty-Eighth Chapter. (SρĦᛁ)

Thus I saw how Christ has compassion on us, for the cause of sin.
And right as I was before in the Passion of Christ fulfilled with
pain and compassion, like in this I was fulfilled in part with compassion of all my even-Christians, for that well-beloved people who shall

be saved. (Ⱨ) Then I saw that each natural compassion that man has of his even-Christian with charity, that is Christ in him. (ꙅꝓꚈ) That is to say, God's servants, holy Church, shall be shaken in sorrow and anguish and tribulation in this world, as men shake a cloth in the wind. And as to this our Lord answered in this manner, "Ah, a great thing shall I make hereof in heaven of endless worship and everlasting joy." Yea, so far as I saw that our Lord joys of the tribulations of his servants, with ruth and compassion. To each person whom he loves to bring to his bliss, he leaves upon them something that is no lack in his sight, whereby they are blamed and despised in this world, scorned, struck, and cast out. And this he does to stop the harm that they should take of the pomp and the vainglory of this wretched life. And make their way ready to come to heaven and exalt them in his bliss lasting without end. For he says, "I shall all break you of your vain affections and your vicious pride and after that I shall gather you together and make you mild and meek, clean and holy, by oneing to me." And then I saw that each natural compassion that man has on his even-Christian with charity, it is Christ in him. That same noughting that was showed in his Passion, was showed again here in this compassion, wherein were two kinds of understandings in our Lord's meaning. The one was the bliss that we are brought to wherein he will be enjoyed. ¶ That other is for comfort in our pain. For he will that we know that it shall all be turned to worship and profit by virtue of his Passion. And that we understand that we do not suffer alone, but with him and see him our ground. And that we see his pains, and his noughting, pass so far all that we may suffer that it may not be fully thought. ¶ And the behold-ing of this will save us from grouching and despair in the feeling of our pains, and if we see truly that our sin deserves it, yet his love excuses us. And of his great courtesy he does away all our blame, and he holds us in ruth and pity as innocent and unloathsome children.

38

(ꙅ) Adam's sin was greatest, but the satisfaction for it is more pleasing to God than ever was the sin harmful. (ꙅꝓ) The Twenty-Ninth Chapter. (ꙅꝓꚈ)

{B} ut in this I stood, beholding generally grieving and mourning, saying thus to our Lord in my meaning with full great dread,

"Ah, good Lord, how might all be well for the great hurt that is come by sin to the creatures." And here I desired as I dared, to have some more open declaring, wherewith I might be eased in this. ¶ And to this our blessed Lord answered full meekly and with full lovely cheer, and showed (Ħ) me (SƿĦ) that Adam's sin was the most harm that ever was done or ever shall be to the world's end. And also he showed (Ħ) me (SƿĦ) that this is as openly known in all holy Church on earth. ¶ Furthermore he taught (Ħ) me (SƿĦ) that I should behold the glorious Satisfaction. For this Assize-making is more pleasing to God and more worshipful for man's salvation without comparison, than ever was the sin of Adam harmful. ¶ Then means our blessed Lord thus, in this teaching, that we should pay heed to this, "For since I have made well the most harm, then it is my will that you know thereby that I shall make well, all that is less."

❧

39

(S) How we should joy and trust in our Saviour Jesus, not presuming to know his privy counsel. (Sƿᴜ) The Thirtieth Chapter. (SƿĦᴜ)

Ħe gave me understanding of two parties. That one part is our Saviour and our Salvation. This blessed part is open and clear and fair and light and plenteous for all mankind that is of good will and shall be, is comprehended in this part. ¶ Hereto are we of God and drawn and enabled and taught inwardly by the holy Ghost and outwardly by the holy Church in the same grace. ¶ In this will our Lord that we be occupied in joying in him, for he enjoys in us. ¶ And the more plenteously that we take of this with reverence and meekness, the more thanks we deserve of him and the more help to ourself. And thus may we say enjoying, "Our part is our Lord." ¶ That other is hid and stored from us, that is to say all that is beside our salvation. For it is our Lord's Privy Counsel, and it belongs to the Royal Lordship of God to have his privy counsel in peace, and it belongs to his servant for obedience and reverence, not to know his counsel well. ¶ Our Lord has pity and compassion on us, for that some creatures make them so busy therein. And I am secure if we knew how much we should please him and ease ourself to believe it, we would. The saints who be in heaven, they will to know nothing, but what our Lord will show them. And also their charity, and their desire is ruled after the will of our Lord.

And thus ought we to will not like to them. ¶ Then shall we will nor desire nothing but the will of our Lord, like as they do. For we are all one in God's meaning. ¶ And here I was taught that we shall trust and enjoy only in our Saviour, blissful Jesus, for all things.

(Ƨ) Of the longing and spiritual thirst of Christ which lasts and shall last until Doomsday. And by the reason of his body he is not yet full glorified nor all immortal. (Ƨ&) The Thirty-First Chapter. (Ƨ&Ⴖ)

{Ⴖ nd thus our good Lord answered to all the questions and doubts that I might make, saying full comfortably, "I may make all things well, I can make all thing well, and I will make all thing well, and I shall make all thing well, and you shall see your self that all manner of thing shall be well." That he says "I may" I understand for the Father and he says "I can" I understand for the Son. ¶ And where he says "I will," I understand for the holy Ghost. ¶ And where he says "I shall" I understand for the Unity of the Blessed Trinity, Three Persons and One Truth. ¶ And where he says, "You shall see yourself," I understand ▨▨▨ the oneing of all mankind who shall be saved into the blissful Trinity. And in these five words God will that we be enclosed in rest and in peace. And thus shall the ghostly thirst of Christ have an end. ¶ For this is the ghostly thirst of Christ, the love longing that lasts and ever shall till we see that sight on Doomsday. For we who shall be saved, and shall be Christ's joy and his bliss, some be yet here, and some be to come. And so shall some be in to that day, therefore this is his thirst, a love-longing to have us all together whole in him to his endless bliss as to my sight, (Ⴖ) the failing of his bliss, that he does not have us in him as wholly as he shall then have. (Ƨ&) ¶ For we be not now as fully as whole in him as we shall be then. For we know in our faith, and also it was showed in all that Christ Jesus is both God and man, and concerning the Godhead he is himself highest bliss, and was from without beginning. And shall be from without end. Which endless bliss may never be heightened nor lowered in the self. ¶ For this was plenteously seen in every Showing and namely in the Twelfth, where he says "I it am who is highest." And concerning Christ's manhood it is known in our faith and also showed that he with the virtue of the Godhead for love to bring us to his bliss, suffered pains and passions,

40

and died. ¶ And these be the works of Christ's manhood wherein he enjoys. And that he showed in the Ninth Revelation, where he says "It is a joy, a bliss, an endless liking to me, that ever I suffered Passion for you." And this is the bliss of Christ's works and thus he means where he says in the self-same Showing, we be his bliss, we be his reward, we be his worship, we be his crown. For concerning that Christ is our head, he is glorified and immortal. And concerning his body in which all his members be knit, he is not yet fully glorified nor yet all immortal. For the same desire and thirst that he had upon the Cross, which desire, longing and thirst, as to my sight, was in him from without beginning, the same he has yet, and shall, until the time that the last soul that shall be saved is come up to his bliss. ¶ For as truly, as there is a property in God of ruth and pity, as truly is there a property in God of thirst and longing. And of the virtue of this longing in Christ, we have to belong again to him, without which no soul comes to heaven. And this property of longing and thirst comes of the endless goodness of God. Right as the property of pity comes of his endless goodness. And though longing and pity are two sundry properties as to my sight. And in this stands the point of the ghostly thirst, which is lasting in him as long as we be in need, drawing us up into his bliss. ¶ And all this was seen in the Showing of compassion. For that shall cease on Doomsday. 🙰 Thus he has ruth and compassion on us. And he has longing to have us, but his wisdom and his love suffer not the end to come till the best time.

41

(S) How all thing shall be well and Scripture fulfilled, and we must steadfastly hold us in the faith of holy Church, as is Christ's will. (spa) The Thirty-Second Chapter.

One time our good Lord said, "All manner of thing shall be well." And another time he said "You shall see yourself that all manner of thing shall be well." And in these two the soul took sundry understanding. One was this, that he will we understand, that not only he pays heed to noble things and to great, but also to little and to small, to low and to simple, to one and to the other. And so means he in that he says "All manner of things shall be well." For he will we know the least thing shall not be forgotten. ¶ Another understanding is this, that there be evil deeds done in our sight and so great harm taken, that it seems to us that it were impossible that ever it should come to a good end. And upon this we look sorrowing and mourning, therefore so that we cannot rest us in the blissful beholding of God as we should do. ¶ And the cause of this, is that the use of our reason is now so blind, so low and so simple, that we cannot know that high marvelous wisdom, the might and the goodness of the blissful Trinity. And thus means he where he says, "You shall see yourself that all manner of thing shall be well." As if he said, "Pay heed now faithfully and trustingly and at the last end you shall truly see it in fullness of joy." ¶ And thus in these same five words beforesaid "I may make all things well, etc.," I understand a mighty comfort of all the works of our Lord God, that are to come. ¶ There is a deed the which the blessed Trinity shall do in the last day, as to my sight, and when the deed shall be and how it shall be done, is unknown of all creatures who are beneath Christ and shall be until when it is done. (♡) The goodness and the love of our Lord God will that we know it shall be. ¶ And the might and the wisdom will of him by the same love heal it and hide it from us, what it shall be and how it shall be done. (♡♡) And the cause he will we know is for he will we be the more eased in our soul and peaced in love, leaving the beholding of all tempests that might stop us of true enjoying in him. ¶ This is that great deed ordained of our Lord God from without beginning, treasured and hid in his blessed breast, only known to himself, by which deed he shall make all things well. ¶ For like as the blessed Trinity made all things of nought, right so the same blessed Trinity shall make well all that is not well. And in this sight I marveled greatly and beheld our faith, marveling thus. Our faith is grounded in God's word, and it belongs to our faith, that we ▨▨▨ believe that God's word shall be saved in all things. ¶ And one point of our faith is that many creatures shall be damned as Angels who fell out of heaven for pride who be now fiends. And men on earth who die outside of the faith of the holy Church, that is to say they who be heathen men. And also men who have received Christendom and live un-Christian lives, and so die out of charity. All these shall be damned to hell without end, as holy Church teaches me to believe. ¶ And given all this, I thought it was impossible that all manner of thing should be well as our Lord showed in the time. And as to this I had no other answer in Showing of our Lord God but this, "What is impossible to you is not impossible to me. I shall save my word in all things and I shall make all thing well." Thus I was taught by the grace of God, that I should steadfastly hold me in the faith as I had beforehand understood. And therewith that I should solemnly believe

that all thing shall be well, as our Lord showed in the same time. For
this is the great deed that our Lord shall do, in which deed he shall save
his word in all thing. And he shall make well all that is not well. (Ꝑ)
But what the deed shall be, (Sꝑ) and how it shall be done there is no
creature beneath Christ who knows it, nor shall know it, till it is done,
as to the understanding that I took of our Lord's meaning in this time.

(S) All damned Souls be despised in the sight of God as the Devil. And
these Revelations withdraw not the faith of holy Church, but comfort.
And the more we busily seek to know God's secrets, the less we know.
(Sꝑ) The Thirty-Third Chapter.

And yet in this I desired as I dared that I might have had full sight
of Hell and Purgatory. But it was not my meaning, to be privy to
anything that belongs to the faith. For I believed truly, that Hell and
Purgatory is for the same end that holy Church teaches, but my meaning was that I might have seen for learning in all things that belong to
my faith, whereby I might live the more to God's worship and to my
profit. And for my desire I learned of this right nought, but as it is
aforesaid in the Fifth Showing, where I saw that the Devil is reproved
by God and endlessly damned. ¶ In which sight I understood that all
creatures who are of the Devil's condition in this life, and therein end,
there is no more mention made of them before God and all his holy
ones than of the Devil, notwithstanding that they be of mankind,
whether they have been Christened or not. For though the Revelation
was made of goodness in which was made little mention of evil, yet
I was not drawn thereby from any point of the faith that holy Church
teaches me to believe. For I had sight of the Passion of Christ in diverse
Showings, in the First, in the Second, in the Fifth, and in the Eighth, as
it is said before. Whereas I had in part a feeling of the sorrow of our
Lady. And of his true friends who saw him in pain. But I saw not so
properly specified the Jews who did him to death, notwithstanding I
knew in my faith that ▩ they were cursed and damned without
end; saving those who converted by grace. ¶ And I was strengthened
and taught generally to keep me in the faith in every point, and in all,
as I had before understood, hoping that I was therein with the mercy
and the grace of God desiring and praying in my meaning that I might

continue therein unto my life's end. ¶ It is God's will that we have great regard to all his deeds that he has done, all that he shall do. But evermore we need to believe the beholding what the deed shall be. And we desire to be like our brethren who be saints in heaven, who will right nought but God's will. Then shall we only enjoy in God, and be well paid both with hiding and with showing. ¶ For I saw truly in our Lord's meaning, the more we busy ourselves to know his secrets in this or any other thing, the farther shall we be from the knowing thereof. (Ħ) And that showed he me in this word that he said, "And you shall see yourself that all manner of thing shall be well." This I understood in two ways. One, that I am well-paid that I knew it not. Another, I am glad and merry, for I shall know it. It is God's will that we should know it all shall be well, in general, but it is not God's will that we should know it now, but as it belongs to us for the time and that is the teaching of holy Church.

(S) God shows the secrets necessary to his Lovers, and how they much please God who receive diligently the preaching of holy Church. (Sᑭ) The Thirty-Fourth Chapter.

Our Lord God showed two kinds of secrets. One is this great secret with all the privy points that belong thereto. And these privities he will we know to be hidden until the time that he will clearly show them to us. That other are the secrets that he will make open and known to us. For he will we know that it is his will we know them. These are secrets to us not only because he wills they been secrets to us, but they are privities to us for our blindness and our unknowing. And thereof he has great ruth. And therefore he will himself make them more open to us, whereby we may know him, and love him and cleave to him. For all that is helpful to us to understand and to know, full courteously will our Lord show us. And that is this with all the preaching and teaching of holy Church. (SᑭĦ) ¶

God showed (Ħ) me (SᑭĦ) full great pleasure that he has in all men and women, who mightily and meekly and wilfully take the preaching and teaching of holy Church. For (S) it is his (Ħ) he is (SᑭĦ) holy Church, ¶ he is the ground, ¶ he is the substance, ¶ he is the teaching, ¶ he is the teacher, ¶ he is the way, ¶ he is the reward, wherefore every soul travails, and this is known and shall be known to every soul to whom the holy Ghost declares it. And I hope truly that all those who seek shall be helped for they seek God. ¶ All this that I have now said, and more that I shall say after is comforting against sin. ¶ For in the Third Showing when I saw that God does all that is done, I saw no sin, and then I saw that all is well, but when God showed me for sin, then he said, "All shall be well."

(S) How God does all that is good and suffers worshipfully all by his mercy, the which shall cease when sin is no longer suffered. (SP) The Thirty-Fifth Chapter. (SPᛝ)

44

And when God Almighty had showed (ᛝ) me (SPᛝ) so plenteously and so fully of his goodness, I desired to know of a certain creature whom I loved, if it should continue in good living, which I hoped by the grace of God was begun (ᛝ) how it should be with her. (SPᛝ) And in this singular desire it seemed that I hindered myself, for I was not taught in this time. And then was I answered in my reason, as it were with a friendly meaning, ¶ "Take it generally and behold the courtesy of the Lord God as he shows to you, for it is more worship to God to behold him in all, than in any special thing." ¶ I assented and therewith I learned that it is more worship to God to know all things in general, than to desire anything in particular. And if I should do wisely after this teaching, I should not only be glad for nothing in special, nor greatly diseased for any manner of thing, for all shall be well. ¶ For the fullness of joy is to behold God in all. ¶ For by the same blessed might, wisdom and love that he made all things, to the same end our good Lord leads it continually, and thereto himself shall bring it, and when it is time we shall see it. And the ground of this was showed in the First Showing and more openly in the Third Showing where it says, ¶ "I saw God in a point." All that our Lord does is rightful and that he suffers is worshipful. ¶ And in these two is comprehended good and ill. ¶ For all that is good our Lord does, and that is evil our Lord suffers. I say not that any evil is worshipful, but I say the suffering of our Lord God is worshipful, whereby his goodness shall be known without end, in his marvelous meekness and mildness by the working of mercy and grace. ¶ Rightfulness is that thing that is so good, that may not be better than it is. For God himself is very rightfulness, and all his works are done rightfully as they are ordained from without beginning, his high might, his high wisdom, his high goodness. And right as he ordained unto the best, right so he works continually and leads it to the same end. And he is ever fully pleased with himself and with all his works. ¶ And the beholding of this blissful accord is full sweet to the soul who sees (Ρ) it (Sρ) by grace. All the souls who shall be saved in heaven without end, be made rightful in the sight of God. And by his own goodness, in which righteousness we are endlessly kept, and marvelously above all creatures. And mercy is a working that comes of the goodness of God. ¶ And it shall last in working all along as sin is suffered to pursue   45 a rightful soul. And when sin has no longer leave to pursue, then shall the working of mercy cease. And then shall all be brought to righteousness and therein stand without end. ¶ And by his sufferance we fall, and in his blissful love with his might and his wisdom we are kept. And by mercy and grace we are raised to manifold more joys. ¶ And thus in righteousness and in mercy he will be known and loved now without end. And the soul who wisely beholds it in grace it is well (S) pleased with both and endlessly enjoys.

(S) Of another excellent deed that our Lord shall do, which by grace may be known in part here. And how we should enjoy in the same. And how God yet does miracles. (Sρ) The Thirty-Sixth Chapter.

Our Lord God showed that a deed shall be done, and himself shall do it. (Ρ) And it shall be worshipful and marvelous and plenteous and by him it shall be done. And he himself shall do it. And this is the highest joy that the soul understands, that God himself shall do it. (Sρ) And I shall do nothing but sin and my sin shall not stop his goodness from working. ¶ And I saw that the beholding of this is a high joy in a dreadful soul, who evermore naturally by grace desires God's will. This deed shall be begun here, and it shall be worshipful to God, and plenteously profitable to his lovers on earth. And ever as we come to heaven we shall see it in marvelous joy. And it shall last thus in working unto the last day. And the worship and the bliss of that shall last in heaven before God and all his holy saints without end. Thus was this deed seen and understood in our Lord's meaning. And the cause why he showed it, is to make us enjoy in him and in all his works. ¶ When I saw his Showing continued, I understood that it was showed for a great thing that was for to come, which thing God showed that himself should do it. Which deed has these properties beforesaid. ¶ And this showed he well blissfully meaning that I should take it wisely, faithfully, and trustingly. But what this deed should be it was kept secret to me. ¶ And in this I saw that he will not that we dread to know the things that he shows. ¶ He shows them for he will we know them, by which knowing he will we love him, and delight and endlessly enjoy in him. And for the great love that he has to us he shows us all that is worshipful, and profitable for the time. And the things that he will now have secret, yet of his great goodness he shows them close. ¶ In which Showing he will we believe and understand, that we shall see it truly in his endless bliss. ¶ Then ought we to enjoy in him, for all that he shows, and all that he hides, and if we wilfully and meekly do thus, we shall find therein great ease, and endless thanks we shall have of him therefore. And thus is the understanding of this word, "That it

46 shall be done by me," that is the general man, that is to ▒▒▒ say all who shall be saved. It shall be worshipful and marvelous and plenteous. And God himself shall do it. And this shall be the highest joy that may be to behold the deed that God himself shall do. And man shall do right nought but sin. ¶ Then means our Lord God thus, as if he said, "Behold and see. Here you have matter of meekness. Here you have matter of love. Here you have matter to nought yourself. Here you have matter to enjoy in me. And for my love enjoy in me. For of all things therewith might you most please me." And as long as we are in this life, what time that we, by our folly, turn us to the beholding of the reproved, tenderly our Lord God touches us, and blissfully calls us, saying in our soul, (ᏢᏳ) "Let me alone," (Ꮥ) "Let be all your love," (ᏕᏢᏳ) "my dearworthy child. Intend to me. I am enough to you. And enjoy in your Saviour and in your salvation." (ᏕᏢ) And that this is our Lord's working in us. I am secure the soul that is pierced therein by grace shall see it and feel it. And though it be so, that this deed be truly taken for the general man, yet it excludes not the particular. For what our good Lord will do by his poor creatures it is now unknown to me. ¶ But this deed and the other aforesaid. They are not both one but two sundry. ¶ But this deed shall be done sooner and that shall be as we come to heaven and to whom our Lord gives it, it may be known here in part. But the great deed beforesaid shall neither be known in heaven nor on earth till it is done. ¶ And moreover he gave special under-

standing and teaching of working and showing of miracles. As thus, ¶ "It is known that I have done miracles here before, many and plenty, high and marvelously worshipful and great. And so as I have done, I do now continually, and shall do in the coming of time." ¶ It is known that before miracles come sorrow and anguish and tribulation, and that is that we should know our own feebleness and our mischief that we are fallen in by sin, to humble us, and to make us dread God, crying for help and grace. And great miracles come after that, and that of the high might, wisdom, and goodness of God, showing his virtue and the joys of heaven, so as it may be in this passing life and that for to strengthen our faith, and to increase our hope in charity. Wherefore it pleases him to be known and worshiped, in miracles. Then he means thus, he will that we be not brought too low through sorrow and tempests that befall us, for it has always been so before miracles coming.

(S) God keeps his chosen full securely although they sin, for in these is a godly will that never tried to sin. (Sp) The Thirty-Seventh Chapter. (SpH) ᚱᛟᛜ

God brought to my mind, that I should sin, and for the delight that I had in beholding him, I attended not readily to that Showing. And our Lord full mercifully waited and gave me grace to understand. And this Showing I took singularly to myself. But by all the gracious comfort that followed, as you shall see, I was taught to take it to (H) so I would pay heed, and then our Lord brought to mind with my sins, the sin of (SpH) all my even-Christians, all in general and nothing in special. ¶ Though (H) {If all (SpH) our Lord showed me I should sin, by me alone is understood all. And in this I conceived a soft dread, and to this our Lord answered, "I keep you full securely." This word was said with more love and secureness and ghostly keeping than I can or may tell. ¶ For as it was showed (H) to me (SpH) that I should sin, right so was the comfort showed (H) to me (SpH) of secureness and keeping for all my even-Christians. ¶ What may make me more to love my even-Christians, than to see in God, that he loves all who shall be saved, as it were all one soul. For in every soul who shall be saved, is a godly will that never assented to sin, nor ever shall. Right as there is a beastly will in the lower part that may will no good, right so there is a godly will in the higher part, which will is so good, that it may never will ill, but ever good. And therefore we are whom he loves, and endlessly we do that that he likes. ¶ And this showed our Lord (Ⱶ) to me (SⱣⱵ) in the wholeness of love that we stand in, in his sight. Yea, that he loves us now as well, while we are here, as he shall do when we are there before his blessed face. ¶ But for failing of love on our part, therefore is all our travail.

(S) Sin of the chosen shall be turned to joy and worship. Example of David, Peter, John of Beverley. (SⱣ) The Thirty-Eighth Chapter. (Ᵽ)

And also God showed (Ⱶ) me (SⱣⱵ) that sin shall be no shame, but worship to man, for right as to every sin is answering a pain by truth, right so for every sin to the same soul is given a bliss by love. Right as diverse sins are punished with diverse pains after that they be grievous, right so shall they be rewarded with diverse joys in heaven, after they have been painful and sorrowful to the soul on earth. For the soul that shall come to heaven is precious to God, and the place so worshipful, that the goodness of God suffers never that soul to sin who shall come there, but sin shall be rewarded. And it is made known without end, and blissfully restored by overpassing honours. ¶ For in this sight my understanding was lifted up into heaven. ¶ And there God brought merrily to my mind David and others in the old law without number. And in the new law he brought to my mind, First Mary Magdalen, Peter and Paul, Thomas and Jude, and Saint John of Beverley. And others also without number, how they are known in the Church on earth with their sins, and it is to them no shame (Ⱶ) that they have sinned, no more it is the bliss of heaven, (SⱣ) but all is turned to their worship. And therefore our courteous Lord showed for them here in part, like as it is there in fullness. For there the tokens of sin are all is turned to their worship. (Ⱶ) Right so our Lord God showed me them in example of all others who shall come there. (SⱣ) ¶ And Saint John of Beverley, our Lord showed him full highly in comfort to us, for homeliness, and brought to my mind how he is a gracious neighbour and of our knowing. And God called him Saint John of Beverley plainly as we do, and that with a full glad sweet cheer, showing that he is a full high saint in heaven in his sight and a blissful one. And with this he

48

made mention that in his youth and in his tender age he was a dear-worthy servant to God, much loving and dreading God. ¶ And never-theless God suffered him to fall, keeping him mercifully so that he perished not nor lost time. ¶ And afterward God raised him to mani-fold more grace and by the contrition and meekness that he had in his living, God has given him in heaven manifold joys overpassing that he should have had if he had not fallen. And that this is true God shows on earth, with plenteous miracles done about his body continually, and all this was to make us glad and merry in love.

(S) Of the sharpness of sin and the goodness of contrition and how our natural Lord will not we despair for often falling. (Sᴘ) The Thirty-Ninth Chapter. (Sᴘꓧ)

S in is the sharpest scourge that any chosen soul may be smitten with, which scourge all severely beats man and woman, annoys him in his own sight, so much so that he thinks himself the while he is not worthy but as to sink into hell, till contrition takes him by the touching of the holy Ghost, and turns the bitterness in hopes of God's mercy. And then begin his wounds to heal, and the soul to quicken, turned into the life of holy Church. ¶ The holy Ghost leads him to con-fession wilfully, to show his sins nakedly and truly with great sorrow, and great shame, that he has defouled the fair image of God. Then he undergoes penance for every sin enjoined by his confessor, who is grounded in holy Church by the teaching of the holy Ghost. (ꓧ) By this medicine ought each sinful soul be healed, and namely of sins that are deadly in the self. (Sᴘ) And this is one meekness that much pleases God. And also bodily sickness of God's sending. And also sorrow and shame from without, and disgust and despite of this world, with all manner of grievance and temptations that he will be cast in, bodily and ghostly. Full preciously our Lord keeps us when it ▨▨▨ seems to us that we are near forsaken and cast away for our sin, and because we see that we have deserved it. And because of meekness that we get hereby, we are raised wholly in God's sight by his grace (ᴘ) and also whom our Lord will, he visits with his special grace (Sᴘ) with so great con-trition, also with compassion and true longing to God. Then they be suddenly delivered of sin and of pain, and taken up to bliss, and made

49

even high saints. ¶ By contrition we are made clean, by compassion we
are made ready, and by true longing to God we are made worthy. These
are three means as I understand whereby that all souls come to heaven,
that is to say who have been sinners in earth and shall be saved. ¶ For
by these medicines it is needful that every soul be healed. Though
he be healed his wounds are seen before God, not as wounds but as
worships. ¶ And so on the contrary wise, as we be punished here with
sorrow and with penance, we shall be rewarded in heaven by the courteous love of our Lord God Almighty, who will that none who comes
there lose his travail in any degree. For he beholds sin as sorrow and
pain to his lovers, in whom he assigns no blame for love. The reward
that we shall receive shall not be little, but it shall be high, glorious and
worshipful, and so shall shame be turned to worship and more joy. (Ⓗ)
And I am secure by my own feeling the more that each natural soul
sees this in the natural and courteous love of God, the loather he is to
sin. (ⓈⓅ) For our courteous Lord wills not that his servants despair, for
often, nor for grievous, falling, for our falling does not stop him from
loving us. ¶ Peace and love are ever in us being and working. But we
be not always in peace and in love. But he will that we take heed thus
that he is ground of all our whole life in love. ¶ And furthermore that
he is our everlasting keeper and mightily defends us against our
enemies, who are full evil and fierce upon us. And so much our need is
the more, for we give him occasion by our falling.

(Ⓢ) We need to belong in love with Jesus, eschewing sin for love. The
vileness of sin passes all pains. And God wholly loves us tenderly while
we be in sin, and so we need to do to our neighbour. (ⓈⓅ) The Fortieth
Chapter.

And this is a sovereign friendship of our courteous Lord, that he
keeps us so tenderly while we be in sin, and furthermore he touches
us full privily and shows us our sin by the sweet light of mercy and
grace. But when we see our self so foul, then we think that God were
wroth with us for our sin. And then we are stirred of the holy Ghost by
contrition into prayers and desire to amend our life, with all our might
to appease the wrath of God until the time we find a rest in soul, and
softness ▨ in conscience. And then we hope that God has forgiven

us our sins. And it is true. ¶ And then shows our courteous Lord himself to the soul wholly merrily and with glad cheer, with friendly welcoming, as if he had been in pain and in prison, saying sweetly thus, "My dear darling, I am glad you are come to me in all your woe. I have ever been with you, and now you see my loving, and we be oned in bliss." Thus are sins forgiven by mercy and grace, and our soul worshipfully received in joy, like as it shall be when it comes to heaven, as oftentimes as it comes by the gracious working of the holy Ghost, and the virtue of Christ's Passion. ¶ Here understood I truly that all manner thing is made ready to us by the great goodness of God, so much that what time we be ourself in peace and charity, we be truly saved. But because we may not have this in fullness while we are here, therefore it befalls us ever the more to live in sweet prayer and in lovely longing with our Lord Jesus. For he longs ever to bring us to the fullness of joy, as it is beforesaid, where he shows the ghostly thirst. (SPꟼ) ¶

{B}ut now because of all this ghostly comfort, that is said before, if any man or woman (ꟼ) if you (SPꟼ) be stirred by folly to say or to think, "If this be true, then were it good to sin to have the more reward," or else to charge the less to the sin, beware of this stirring (ꟼ) and despise it for it is (SP) for truly if it come it is a lie, and (SPꟼ) of the enemy. (SP) ¶ For the same true love that teaches us all this comfort, the same blessed love teaches us that we should hate sin only for love. (ꟼ) For what soul who wilfully takes this stirring he may never be saved till he makes amends for deadly sin. (SP) ¶ And I am sure by my own feeling, the more that every natural soul sees this in the courteous love of our Lord God, the loather is he to sin. And the more he is ashamed. (SPꟼ) For if were laid before us all the pains in hell and in purgatory and on earth, death and other, and sin, we should rather choose all that pain than sin. ¶ For sin is so vile and so much to hate that it may be like to no pain which pain is not sin. ¶ And to me was showed no harder hell than sin. For a natural soul has no hell but sin. (ꟼꟼ) For all is good but sin, and nought is (ꟼ) evil (ꟼ) wicked (ꟼꟼ) but sin. (ꟼ) Sin is neither deed nor desire. But when a soul chooses sin wilfully, that is pain before his God. At the end he has right nought. That pain, I think, the hardest Hell. For he has not his God. In all pains a soul may have God but in sin. (SP) ¶ And we, given our intent to love and meekness by the working of mercy and grace, we are made all fair and clean. And as mighty, and as wise as God is to save man, as willing he is. ¶ For Christ himself is ground of all the laws of Christian men. And he taught us to do good against ill evil. Here may we see that he is himself this charity, and does to us as he teaches us to do, for he will we be like him in wholeness of endless love to our self and to our even-Christians. No more then is his love broken to us, for our sin; no more will he that our love be broken to ourself and to our even-Christian, but nakedly hate sin and endlessly love the soul as God loves it. Then shall we hate sin, like as God hates it, and love the soul as God loves it. For this word that is said is an endless comfort, "I keep you full truly." (S℘)

51

The Fourteenth Revelation (S) is as said before, etc. It is impossible we should pray for mercy and want it. And how God wills that we always pray though we be dry and barren, for that prayer is to him acceptable and pleasing. (S℘) The Forty-First Chapter. (ⱲS℘Ħ)

{Ħ} fter this our Lord showed (Ħ) to me (ⱲS℘) for (Ħ) four (ⱲS℘Ħ) prayers. In which Showing I see two conditions in our Lord's meaning, (Ħ) in them who pray, as I have felt in myself (ⱲS℘) ¶ One is rightfulness. ¶ Another is secure trust. (Ħ) One is they will pray not just for anything that may be, but only what is God's will and his worship. Another is that they set them mightily and continually to ask that thing that is his will and his worship. And this is as I have understanding by the teaching of holy Church. For in this our Lord taught me the same, to have of God's gift faith, hope, and charity, And to keep us therein to our lives' end. And in this we say **Pater Noster, Ave,** and **Credo,** with devotion as God will give it. And thus we pray for all our even-Christians and for all manner of men what God's will is. For we would that all manner of men and women were in the same virtue and grace that we ought to desire for our self. (ⱲS℘Ħ) But yet oftentimes our trust is not full for we are not secure that God hears us as we think, for our unworthiness and because we feel right nought. For we are as barren and dry oftentimes after our prayers as we were before, and this in our feeling. Our folly is cause of our weakness, for thus have I felt in myself. ¶ And all this brought our Lord suddenly to my mind, (Ħ) and mightily and lively and comforting me against this kind of weakness in prayers. (ⱲS℘) And showed these words and said, "I am ground of your prayer. First it is my will that you have it, and since I make you to will, and since I make you to beseech it, and you beseech it, how should it then be that you should not have your beseeching?" And thus in the first reason with the three that follow, our good Lord shows a mighty comfort as it may be seen in the same words. And in the first reason thus he says, "And you pray it," there he shows the full great pleasance and endless reward that he will give us for our beseeking, and in the sixth reason there he says, "How should it then be, (A) that you should not have your beseeching?" There he shows a sober undertaking for we trust not as mightily as we should. Thus will our Lord that we both pray and trust. For the cause of the reasons beforesaid is to make us strong against weakness in our prayers. For it is God's will we pray and thereto he stirs us in these words beforesaid. For he will that we be secure to have our prayer. For prayer pleases God. Prayer pleases man with himself and makes him sober and meek who beforehand was in strife and travail. This was said for an impossibility. For it is the most impossible that that may be that we should beseech mercy and grace and not have it. ¶ For of all thing that our good Lord makes us to beseech himself has ordained it to us from without beginning. Here may we see that our beseeking is not cause of God's goodness and grace that he does to us. ¶ And that showed he truthfully in all these sweet words, when he says, "I am ground of your prayer and of your requests." And our good Lord wills that this be known of his lovers on earth. ¶ And the more that we know, the more should we beseech if it be wisely taken and so is our Lord's meaning. Beseeching is a true gracious lasting will of the soul, oned and fastened into the will of our Lord by the sweet privy work of the holy Ghost. ¶ Our Lord himself, he is the first receiver of our prayers as to my sight, and takes it full thankfully and highly enjoying and he sends it up above, and sets it in a treasury where it shall never perish. It is there before God with all his holy company, continually received, ever helping our needs. ¶ And when we shall receive ▨▨▨ our bliss, it shall be given us for a degree of joy with endless worshipful thanking of him. Full glad and merry is our Lord of our prayer and he looks thereafter and he will have it. For with his grace he makes us like to himself in condition, as we are in nature. And so is his blissful will. ¶ For he says thus, "Pray entirely inwardly, though you think it savours you not. For it is profitable, though you feel not, though you see nought, Yea, though you think you might not, for in dryness and in barrenness, in sickness and in feebleness, then is your prayer well pleasing to me, though you think it savour you not but little. And so is your believing living prayer in my sight." For the reward and the endless thanks that he will give

52

us, therefore he is covetous to have us pray continually in his sight. ¶ God accepts the good will and the travail of this servant, howsoever we feel. Wherefore it pleases him that we work and in our prayers and in good living by his help, and his grace, reasonably with discretion keeping our mights to him, till when we have him whom we seek in fullness of joy who is Jesus. And that showed he in the Fifth Showing, before this word, "You shall have me to your reward." And also to prayers belong thanksgiving. Thanking is a true inward knowing with great reverence and lovely dread, turning our self with all our mights into the working that our good Lord stirs us to enjoying and thanking inwardly. And sometimes for plenteousness it breaks out with voice and says, "Good Lord, grant mercy. Blessed must you be." And sometimes when the heart is dry and feels nought or else by temptation of the enemy, then it is driven by reason and by grace to cry upon our Lord with voice rehearsing his blessed Passion and his great goodness. And the virtue of our Lord's word turns into the soul, and quickens the heart, and enters it by his grace into true working. And makes it pray well blissfuly and truly to enjoy our Lord. It is a full blissful thanking in his sight.

(S) Of three things that belong to prayer, and how we should pray and of the goodness of God who complements us always in our imperfection and feebleness, when we do what belongs to us to do. (Sp) The Forty-Second Chapter. (Wsp)

Our Lord God wills that we have true understanding and namely in three things that belong to our prayers. The first is by whom, and how our prayers spring. ⟨⟩ By whom he shows when he says, "I am ground," and how by his goodness. For he says, "First it is my will." For the second, in what manner and how we should use our prayers, and that is that our will be turned into the will of our Lord enjoying. And so means he when he says, "I make you to will it." For the third, that we know the fruit and the end of our prayers, that is to be oned and like to our Lord in all thing. And to this meaning and for this end was all this lovely lesson showed. And he will help us and we shall make it so as he says himself, Blessed must he be. ¶ For this is our Lord's will, that our prayers and our trust be both alike large. For if we

53

trust not as much as we pray, we do not full worship to our Lord in our prayers. And also we tarry and pain ourself. And the cause is, as I believe, for we know not truly that our Lord is ground on whom our prayer springs. And also that we know not, that it is given us by the grace of his love. For if we knew this, it would make us to trust to have of our Lord's gift all that we desire. ¶ For I am secure, that no man asks mercy and grace, with true meaning but mercy and grace be first given to him. ¶ But sometimes it comes to our mind, that we have prayed a long time, and yet we think, that we have not our asking. But for this we should not be heavy. For I am secure by our Lord's meaning, that either we abide a better time, or more grace, or a better gift. ¶ He will we have true knowing in himself that he is being. And in this knowing he will that our understanding be grounded with all our mights, and all our intent, and all our meaning and in this ground he will that we take our homestead and our dwelling, and by the gracious light of himself, he will we have understanding of the things that follow. ¶ The first is our noble and excellent making. ¶ The second, our precious and dearworthy again-buying. ¶ The third, all thing that he has made beneath us, to serve us, and for our love keeps it. Then means he thus as if he said, ¶ "Behold and see that I have done all this, before your prayers, and now you are, and pray to me." And thus he means, that it belongs to us to know that the greatest deeds be done as holy Church teaches. ¶ And in the beholding of this with thanking we ought to pray for the deed that is now in doing, and that is, that he rule us and guide us to his worship in this life, and bring us to his bliss, and therefore he has done all. ¶ Then means he thus, that we see that he does it. And we pray therefore. For that one is not enough, for if ▨▨ we pray and see not that he does it, it makes us heavy, and doubtful, and that is not his worship. And if we see that he does, and we pray not, we do not our debt, and so may it not be, that is to say, so is it not in his beholding. But to see that he does it, and to pray forthwith so is he worshiped and we helped. ¶ All thing that our Lord has ordained to do, it is his will that we pray therefore either in special or in general. And the joy and the bliss that it is to him, and the thanking and the worship that we shall have therefore, it passes the understanding of creatures as to my sight. ¶ For prayer is a righteous understanding of that fullness of joy that is for to come with true longing and secure trust. Failing of our bliss that we be ordained to naturally makes us to long. For true understanding and love with sweet mind in our Saviour graciously makes us for to trust. Thus we have of nature to long and grace to trust. ¶ And in these

54

two workings our Lord beholds us continually. For it is our debt and his goodness may no less assign in us. Then it belongs to us to do our diligence. And when we have done it, then shall we yet think that it is nought, and truly it is. But do we as we may and truly ask mercy and grace, all that fails us we shall find in him. And thus he means where he says, "I am ground of your beseeching." And thus in this blissful word with the Showing I saw a full overcoming against all our weakness, and all our doubtful dreads.

(S) What prayer does, ordained to God's will. And how the goodness of God has great liking in the deeds that he does by us, as he were beholden to us, working all things sweetly. The Forty-Third Chapter. (SPꓧ)

Prayer ones the soul to God. For though the soul be ever like to God in nature and substance restored by grace, it is often unlike in condition by sin on man's part. Then is prayer a witness that the soul will as God will, (ꓧ) and then it is like to God in condition as it is in kind. (SP) And comforts the conscience and enables man to grace. And thus he teaches us to pray, and mightily to trust that we shall have it. For all thing that is done, should be done though we never pray it. For he beholds us in love, and will make us partner of his good deed. ¶ And therefore he stirs us to pray, that which he delights to do. ¶ For which prayers and good will that he will have of his gift, he will reward us, and give us endless reward. And this was showed (ꓧ) me (SPꓧ) in this word, "And you pray it." ¶ In this word God showed (ꓧ) me (SPꓧ) so great pleasance and so great liking as he were much beholden to us for every good deed that we do, and yet it is he who does it. And for that we beseech him mightily to do all thing that he likes. As if he said, "How might you then please me more, than to beseech mightily, wisely, and wilfully to do that thing that I shall do." ¶ And thus the soul ⬛ by prayer accords between God (ꓧ) and man's soul. (SP) ¶ But when our courteous Lord of his grace shows himself to our soul, we have what we desire. And then we see not for the time that we should pray more, but all our intent with all our might is set wholly to the beholding of him. ¶ And this is a high unperceivable prayer as to my sight. For all the cause wherefore we pray it is oned

into the sight and beholding of him to whom we pray, marvelously enjoying with reverent dread, and so great sweetness and delight in him,
that we can pray right nought but as he stirs us for the time. (Ⴙ) For
what time a man's soul is homely with God he needs not to pray but
behold reverently what he says. For in all this time that this was
showed me I was not stirred to pray, but always to have this well in my
mind for comfort. That when we see God, we have what we desire and
then we need not pray. (ⱲSⱣ) ¶ And well I know the more the soul
sees of God, the more it desires him by his grace. But when we see him
not so, then feel we need and cause to pray for failing, for enabling ourself to Jesus. ¶ For when the soul is tempested, troubled, and left to
himself by unrest, then it is time to pray to make himself supple and
pliant to God. But he by no manner of prayer makes God supple to
him, for he is ever alike in love. (Ⴙ) But in the time that man is in sin he
is so weak, so unwise, and so unloving, that he can neither love God
nor himself. The most mischief that he has is blindness. For he sees not
all this. Then the whole love of God Almighty who ever is one, gives
him sight to himself. Then he understands that God was wroth with
him for his sin and then he is stirred to contrition and by confession
and other good deeds to slake the wrath of God until the time he finds
rest in the soul and softness in conscience. And then he thinks that God
has forgiven him his sins and it is true. And then is God (in the sight of
the soul), turned into the beholding of the soul as if it had been in pain
or prison, saying thus, "I am glad that you are come to rest. For I have
ever loved you and now love you and you me." And thus with prayers,
as I have said before and with other good works that are customary by
the teaching of holy Church is the soul oned to God. (ⱲSⱣ) ¶ And
thus I saw that what time we see needs wherefore we pray, then our
good Lord follows us, helping our desire. And when we of his special
grace plainly behold him, seeing no other needs, then we follow him,
and he draws us into him by love. For I saw and felt that his marvelous
and fulsome goodness fulfills all our mights. ¶ And then I saw that his
continual working in all manner thing is done so godly, so wisely, and
so mightily, that it overpasses all our imagining, and all that we can
understand and think. And then we can do no more but behold him,
enjoying with a high mighty desire to be all oned into him and entered
to his dwelling and enjoy in his loving, and delight in his goodness.
And then shall we with his sweet grace, in our own meek continuing
prayers, come into him now in this life by many privy touchings of
sweet ghostly sights and feeling measured to us as our simpleness may

bear it. ¶ And this is wrought, and shall, by the grace of the holy Ghost so long till we shall die in longing for love. And then shall we all come into our Lord, ourself clearly knowing and God fulsomely having. ¶ And we endlessly be all had in God, him truly seeing, and fulsomely feeling, him ghostly hearing, and him delectably smelling, and him sweetly swallowing, and then shall we see God face to face homely and fulsomely. The creature who is made shall see and endlessly behold God who is the Maker. ¶ For thus may no man see God and live after, that is to say, in this deadly life. But when he of his special grace will

55a show him here, he strengthens the creature 🔲 above the self, and he measures the Showing after his own will as it is profitable for the time.

(S) Of the properties of the Trinity and how man's soul, a creature, has the same properties doing that it was made for, beholding and marveling his God so by that it seems as nought to the self. (Sᑭ) The Forty-Fourth Chapter.

God showed in all the Revelations often, that man works evermore his will and his worship lastingly without any stinting. And what this work is was showed in the First Showing, and that in a marvelous ground. ¶ For it was showed in the working of the soul of our blissful Lady Saint Mary, by Truth and Wisdom. And how I hope by the grace of the holy Ghost, I shall say as I saw. (ᛖᏕᑭ) ¶ Truth sees God, and Wisdom beholds God, and of these two comes the third, that is a holy marvelous delight in God who is Love. Where Truth and Wisdom are verily there is Love, truly coming of them both, and all of God's making. ¶ For he is endless sovereign truth, endless sovereign wisdom, endless sovereign love unmade. And man's soul is a creature in God, who has the same properties made. And evermore it does as it was made for. It sees God, it beholds God, and it loves God. Whereof God enjoys in the creature, and the creature in God endlessly marveling. ¶ In which marveling he sees his God, his Lord, his Maker, so high, so great, and so good in regard of him who is made, that scarce the creature seems ought to the self, but the clearness and the cleanness of truth and wisdom makes him to see, and to be known that he is made for love, in which God endlessly keeps him.

(S) Of the form and deep judgment of God and the variant judgment of man. (SP) The Forty-Fifth Chapter.

God judges us upon our natural substance which is ever kept one in him, whole and saved without end. And this judgment is of his rightfulness. And man judges upon our changeable sensuality, which seems now one, now another, after it takes of the parties and shows outward. And this wisdom is mixed, for sometimes it is good and easy, and sometimes it is hard and grievous. ¶ And inasmuch as it is good and easy it belongs to rightfulness. And in as much as it is hard and grievous, our good Lord Jesus reforms it by mercy and grace, through the virtue of his blessed Passion, and so brings it into the rightfulness. ¶ And though these two be thus accorded and oned, yet it shall be known both in heaven without end. ¶ The first judgment, which is of God's rightfulness, and that is of his high endless life. And this is that fair sweet judgment that was showed in all the fair Revelation in which I saw him assign to us no manner of blame. ¶ And though this was sweet and delectable, yet only in the beholding of this I could not be full eased. And that was for the judgment of holy Church, which I had before understood, and was continually in my sight. ¶ And therefore by this judgment, I thought I needed to know myself a sinner, and by the same judgment, I understood that sinners are worthy sometimes of blame and wrath. And these two I could not see in God. ¶ And there my desire was more than I can or may tell. For the higher judgment God showed himself in the same time. And therefore I needed to take it. And the lower judgment was taught me before in holy Church, and therefore I might in no way leave the lower judgment. ¶ Then was this my desire, that I might see in God, in what manner that the judgment of holy Church herein teaches is true in his sight, and how it belongs to me truly to know it, whereby they might both be saved, so as it were worshipful to God and right way to me. And to all this I had no other answer but a marvelous example of a Lord and of a servant, as I shall say after, and that full mightily showed. And yet I stand in desire and will unto my life's end, that I might by grace know these two judgments, as it belongs to me. ¶ For all heavenly and all earthly things that belong to heaven are comprehended in these two judgments. ¶ And the more understanding by the gracious leading of the holy Ghost that we

have of these two judgments, the more we shall see and know our fail-
ings. And ever the more that we see them, the more naturally by grace
we shall long to be fulfilled of endless joy and bliss for we are made
thereto, and our natural substance is now blissful in God and has been
since it was made, and shall be without end.

(S) We cannot know ourself in this life, but by faith and grace, but we
must know ourself sinners. And how God is never wroth, being most
near the Soul, keeping it. (Sp) The Forty-Sixth Chapter.

But our passing life that we have here in our sensuality knows not
what our self is but in our faith. And when we know and see truly
and clearly what our self is, then shall we truly and clearly see and
know our Lord God in fullness of joy. ¶ And therefore it is needful that
the nearer we be to our bliss, the more we shall long, and that both by
nature and by grace. ¶ We may have knowing of our self in this life, by
continual help and virtue of our high nature, in which knowing we
may increase and grow by nurturing and helping of mercy and grace,
But we may never fully know our self into the last point. In which point
this passing life and manner of pain and woe shall have an end. And
therefore it belongs properly to us both by nature and by grace to
long and desire with all our mights to know ourself, in which knowing
we shall truly and clearly know our God in fulness of endless joy. ¶
And yet in all this time from the beginning to the end I had two manner
of beholding. That one was endless continual love with secureness of
keeping and blissful salvation. For of this was all the Showing. ¶ That
other was the common teaching of holy Church in which I was before
informed and grounded, and wilfully having in use and understanding. And the beholding of this came not from me. For by the Showing
I was not stirred nor led there from in any point, but I had therein
teaching to love it and like it, whereby I might, by the help of our Lord
and his grace, increase and rise to more heavenly knowing and higher
loving. ¶ And thus in all this beholding I thought it needful to see and
to know that we are sinners, and do many evil deeds that we ought to
leave, and leave many good deeds undone that we ought to do, wherefore we deserve pain and wrath. And notwithstanding all this, I saw
truly that our Lord was never wroth and never shall be. ¶ For he is

57

God, good, life, truth, love, peace. His charity, and his unity, suffer him not to be wroth. ¶ For I saw truly that it is against the property of might to be wroth, and against the property of his wisdom, and against the property of his goodness. ¶ God is the goodness who may not be wroth, for he is nought but goodness. Our soul is oned to him, unchangeable goodness, and between God and our soul is neither wrath nor forgiveness in his sight. ¶ For our soul is fulsomely oned to God of his own goodness, that between God and our soul may be right nought. ¶ And to this understanding was the soul led by love, and drawn by might in every Showing. That it is thus, our good Lord showed, and how it is thus, truly of his great goodness, and he will we desire to know, that is to say as it belongs to his creature to know it. ¶ For all thing that the simple soul understands, God wills that it be showed and known. For the things that he will have privy, mightily and wisely he himself hides them for love. ¶ For I saw in the same Showing that much privity is hid, which may never be known until the time that God of his goodness has made us worthy to see it. And therewith I am well paid, abiding our Lord's will in this high marvel. And now I yield me to my mother holy Church as a simple child ought.

(SP) The Forty-Seventh Chapter.

Two points belong to our soul by debt. ¶ One is that we reverently marvel. ¶ That other is that we meekly suffer, ever enjoying in God. For he will that we know that we shall in short time see clearly in himself all that we desire. ¶ And notwithstanding all this, I beheld and marveled greatly, what is the mercy and forgiveness of God? For by the teaching that I had before, I understood that the mercy of God should be the forgiveness of his wrath after the time that we have sinned. ¶ For I thought to a soul whose meaning and desire is to love, that the wrath of God were harder than any other pain. And therefore I took that the forgiveness of his wrath, should be one of the principal points of his mercy. ¶ But for nought that I might behold and desire I could not see this point in all the Showing. ¶ But how I understood and saw of the works of mercy I shall say something as God will give me grace. I understood this, ¶ man is changeable in this life, and by frailty and overcoming falls into sin. He is weak and unwise of himself, and also his will is overlaid, and in this time he is in tempest and in sorrow and woe. And the cause is blindness, for he sees not God. For if he saw God continually, he should have no mischievous feeling, nor any manner of stirring of the yearning that serves to sin. ¶ Thus I saw and felt in the same time. And I thought that the sight and the feeling was high and plenteous, and gracious in regard that our common feeling is in this life. But yet I thought it was but small and low in regard of the great desire that the soul has to see God. ¶ For I felt in myself five ways of working, which be these: Enjoying; mourning; desire; dread; and (S) secure (P) true (SP) hope. ¶ Enjoying, for God gave me understanding, and knowing that it was himself that I saw. ¶ Mourning, and that was for failing. ¶ Desire, and that was that I might see him ever more and more. ¶ Understanding, and knowing, that we shall never have full rest, till we see him truly and clearly, in heaven. ¶ Dread was, for it seemed to me in all that time, that that sight should fail, and I be left to myself. ¶ Secure hope was in the endless love that I saw I should be kept by his mercy, and brought to his bliss. ¶ And the joying in his sight with this secure hope of his merciful keeping made me to have feeling and comfort, so that mourning and dread were not greatly painful. ¶ And yet in all this I beheld in the Showing of God, that this kind of sight of him may not be continual in this life, and that for his own worship, and for increase of our endless joy. And therefore we fail often of the sight of him, and soon we fall 〖JOY〗 into our self and then we find no feeling of right nought, but contrariousness that is in our self. ¶ And that of the elder root of our first sin with all that follows of our contrivance and in this we are travailed, and tempested with feeling of sins and of pains, in many diverse ways, ghostly and bodily, as known to us in this life.

(S) Of mercy and grace and their properties, and how we shall enjoy that we ever suffered woe patiently. (SP) The Forty-Eighth Chapter.

But our good Lord the holy Ghost who is endless life, dwelling in our soul, full securely keeps us and works therein a peace and brings it to ease, by grace, and accords it to God and makes it pliant. And this is the mercy and the way that our Lord continually leads us in as long as we be here in this life, which is changeable. ¶ For I saw no wrath but in man's part, and that he forgives in us. For wrath is not else but a forwardness and a contrariousness to peace and to love. And either it comes of failing of might or of failing of wisdom or of failing of goodness, which failing is not in God, but it is on our part, for we by sin and wrath have in us a wretched and continuous contrariousness to peace and to love. And that showed he most often in his lovely cheer of ruth and pity. ¶ For the ground of mercy is love, and the working of mercy is our keeping in love. And this was showed in such manner, that I could not perceive of the property of mercy otherwise, but as it were alone in love, that is to say as to my sight. ¶ Mercy is a sweet gracious working in love mixed with plenteous pity. For mercy works keeping us, and mercy works turning to us all thing to good. Mercy by love suffers us to fail by measure. ¶ And in as much as we fail, in so much we fall and in as much as we fall, in so much we die. ¶ For we must die, in as much as we fail sight and feeling of God who is our life. ¶ Our failing is dreadful, our falling is shameful, and our dying is sorrowful. ¶ But in all this the sweet eye of pity and love never leaves us nor ceases the working of mercy. For I beheld the property of mercy. And I beheld the property of grace, which have two ways of working in one love. Mercy is a pitiful property which belongs to the Motherhood in tender love. And grace is a worshipful property, which belongs to the royal Lordship in the same love. Mercy works, keeping, suffering, quickening, and healing. And all is of tenderness of love. And grace works, raising, rewarding, and endlessly overpassing, that our loving and our travail deserve spreading abroad, and showing the high plenteous generousness of ▨ God's royal Lordship in his marvelous courtesy. And this is of the abundance of love. For grace works our dreadful failing into plenteous endless solace. ¶ And grace works our shameful falling into high worshipful rising. And grace works our sorrowful dying into holy blissful life. ¶ For I saw full securely that ever as our contrariousness works to us here on earth pain, shame, and sorrow, right so on the contrary wise, grace works to us in heaven, solace, worship, and bliss, and overpassing, so much that when we come up and receive the sweet reward which grace has wrought to us, then we shall thank and bless our Lord endlessly joying, that ever we suffered woe. And that shall be for a property of blessed love, that we shall know in God, which we might never have known without woe going before. ¶

60

And when I saw all this I needed to grant that the mercy of God and the forgiveness is to slacken and lessen our wrath.

(**S**) Our life is grounded in love, without which we perish, but yet God is never wroth, but in our wrath and sin he mercifully keeps us, and treats us to peace, rewarding our tribulations. (**Sp**) The Forty-Ninth Chapter.

For this was a high marvel to the soul who was continually showed in all and with great diligence beholds that our Lord God regarding himself, may not forgive. ¶ For it were impossible that he be wroth. For this was showed that our life is all grounded and rooted in love, and without love we may not live. And therefore to the soul that of his special grace sees so much of the high marvelous goodness of God, and that we are endlessly oned to him in love. It is the most impossible that may be that God should be wroth. ¶ For wrath and friendship be two contraries. For he who lessens and destroys our wrath, and makes us meek and mild, it must needs be that he be ever in one love, meek and mild, which is contrarious to wrath. ¶ For I saw full securely that where our Lord appears, peace is taken and wrath has no place. For I saw no manner of wrath in God, neither for a short time, nor for long. For truly as to my sight, if God might be wroth a touch we should never have life nor stead nor being. For truly as we have our being of the endless might of God, and of the endless wisdom, and of the endless goodness, as truly we have our keeping in the endless might of God, in the endless wisdom, and in the endless goodness. ¶ For though we feel in us wretches, debates and [[?]] strifes, yet are we in all ways enclosed in the mildness of God and in his meekness, in his benignity and in his suppleness. ¶ For I saw full securely that all our endless friendship, our stead, our life, and our being is in God. For that same endless goodness that keeps us when we sin, that we perish not, the same endless goodness continually treats in us a peace against our wrath and our contrarious falling, and makes us to see our need with a true dread mightily to seek into God to have forgiveness with a gracious desire of our salvation. For we may not be blissfully saved till we be truly in peace and in love. For that is our salvation. ¶ And though we, by the wrath and the contrariousness that is in us, be now in tribulation, disease, and woe, as falls to our blindness and frailty, yet are we surely safe by the merciful keeping of God, that we perish not. But we are not blissfully saved in having of our endless joy till we be all in peace and in love, that is to say, full pleased with God and with all his works. And with all his judgments, and loving and peaceable with our self, and with our even-Christian and with all whom God loves as love likes. And this does God's goodness in us. ¶ Thus saw I that God is our true peace. And he is our secure keeper when we are ourselves in unpeace. And he continually works to bring us into endless peace. And thus when we by the working of mercy and grace be made meek and mild, we are full safe. ¶ Suddenly is the soul oned to God, when it is truly peaced in the self for in him is found no wrath. ¶ And thus I saw when we are all in peace and in love, we find no contrariousness, nor no manner of stopping the contrariousness which is now in us. Our Lord of his goodness makes it to us full profitable. For that contrariousness is cause of our tribulations and all our woe. And our Lord Jesus takes them and sends them up to heaven, and there are they made more sweet and delectable than heart may think or tongue may tell. And when we come there we shall find them already turned into very fair and endless worships. ¶ Thus is God our steadfast ground, and he shall be our full bliss and make us unchangeable as he is when we are there.

(S) How the chosen soul was never dead in the sight of God and of a marvel upon the same. And three things made her bold to ask of God understanding of them. (Sp) The Fiftieth Chapter.

And in this deadly life mercy and forgiveness is our way, and evermore lead us to grace. And by the tempest and the sorrow that we fall in on our ▨▨ part we be often dead as to man's judgment on earth. But in the sight of God the soul that shall be saved was never dead nor never shall be. ¶ But yet here I wondered and marveled with all the diligence of my soul, meaning thus, "Good Lord, I see you are very truth and I know truly that we sin grievously all day and be much blameworthy. And I may neither leave the knowing of this truth, nor may I see you showing to us no manner of blame. ¶ How may this be? For I know by the common teaching of holy Church and by my own feeling, that the blame of our sin continually hangs upon us from the

62

first man unto the time that we come up into heaven." ¶ Then was this my marvel that I saw our Lord God showing to us no more blame, than if we were as clean and as holy as angels be in heaven. And between these two contraries my reason was greatly travailed by my blindness, and could have no rest for dread that his blessed presence should pass from my sight, and I be left in unknowing how he beholds us in our sin. ¶ For either I needed to see in God, that sin were all done away, or else I needed to see in God, how he sees it, whereby I might truly know how it belongs to me to see sin, and the manner of our blame. ¶ My longing he endured continually beholding, and yet I could have no patience for great awe and perplexity, thinking if I take it thus that we be not sinners nor not blameworthy, it seems as I should err and fail in knowing of this truth. And if it be so that we be sinners and blameworthy, "Good Lord, how may it then be that I cannot see this truth in you who are my God, my Maker, in whom I desire to see all truths?" For three points make me bold to ask it. ¶ The first is for it is so low a thing, for if it were a high one, I should have been adread. ¶ The second that it is so common, for if it were special and privy, also I should have been afraid. ¶ The third is that I need to know it as I think if I shall live here for knowing of good and evil, whereby I may by reason and grace the more divide them asunder, and love goodness and hate evil as holy Church teaches. ¶ I cried inwardly with all my might seeking unto God for help, meaning thus, "Ah, Lord Jesus, King of Bliss, how shall I be eased? Who shall teach me and tell me what I need to know if I may not

62a   at this time see it in you?" ⟨⟩

(S) The answer to the previous doubt by a marvelous Parable of a Lord and a Servant. And God will be waited for, for it was twenty years after before she fully understood this example. And how it is understood that Christ sits on the right hand of the Father. (Sp) The Fifty-First Chapter.

And then our Courteous Lord answered in showing full mistily a wonderful parable of a Lord who has a servant, and gave me sight to my understanding of both. Which sight was showed double in the Lord. And the sight was showed double in the servant. ¶ Then one part was showed ghostly in bodily likeness. ¶ And the other part was showed more ghostly, without bodily likeness. ¶ For the first thus I saw two persons in bodily likeness, that is to say a Lord and a servant. And therewith God gave me ghostly understanding. The Lord sits solemnly in rest, and in peace. The servant stands before his Lord reverently ready to do his Lord's will. The Lord looks upon his servant full lovely and sweetly and meekly. He sends him to a certain place to do his will. The servant, not only he goes, but suddenly he starts and runs in great haste, for love to do his Lord's will, and immediately he falls into an abyss. And takes full great sore. And then he groans and moans and wails and writhes, but he may not rise nor help himself in any way. ¶ And of all this the most mischief that I saw him in, was failing of comfort, for he could not turn his face to look up on his loving Lord, who was to him full near, in whom is full comfort, but as a man who was feeble and unwise. For the time he attended to his feeling, and endured in woe. In which woe he suffered seven great pains. ¶ The first was the sore bruising that he took in his falling, which was to him feelable pain. ¶ The second was the heaviness of his body. ¶ The third was feebleness following of these two. ¶ The fourth that he was blinded in his reason and shattered in his mind so much that he had almost forgotten his own love. ¶ The fifth was that he might not rise. ¶ The sixth was most marvelous to me and that was that he lay alone. I looked all about and beheld, and far nor near, high nor low, I saw for him no help. ¶ The seventh was that the place which he lay on, was long, hard, and grievous. ¶ I marveled how this servant might meekly suffer there all this woe. And I beheld attentively to know if I could perceive in him any fault, or if the Lord should assign in him any blame. And truly there was none seen. For only his good will and his great desire was cause of his falling. And he was as unloathsome and as good inwardly, as when he stood before his Lord, ready to do his will. And right thus continually his loving Lord full tenderly beholds him. And now with a double cheer, one outward, full meekly and mildly with 🔲 great ruth and pity. And this was of the first. ¶ Another inward more ghostly and this was showed with a leading of my understanding into the Lord which I saw him highly enjoying. For the worshipful resting and nobleness that he will and shall bring his servant to by his plenteous grace. And this was of that other Showing. And now my understanding led again into the first, keeping both in mind. ¶ Then says this courteous Lord in his meaning, "Lo, lo, my loved servant, what harm and disease he has taken in my service for my love. Yea, and for his good will. Is it not reason that I reward him for his fear and his dread, his hurt and his

63

maiming and all his woe. And not only this but falls it not to me to give a gift that be better to him and more worshipful than his own wholeness should have been and else I would think I did him no grace." And in this an inward ghostly showing of the Lord's meaning descended into my soul. In which I saw that it needs must be, given his great and his own worship, that his dearworthy servant whom he loved so much should be truly and blissfully rewarded without end, above what he should have been if he had not fallen. Yea, and so much that his falling and his woe that he has taken thereby, shall be turned to high and overpassing worship and endless bliss. ¶ And at this point the Showing of the example vanished and our good Lord led forth my understanding in sight and in Showing of the Revelation to the end. But notwithstanding all this forthleading, the marveling of the example came never from me. For I thought it was given to me for an answer to my desire. And yet could I not take therein full understanding to my ease at that time. ¶ For in the servant that was showed for Adam as I shall say, I saw many diverse properties that might by no manner be right to the one Adam. And thus in that time I stood much in unknowing. For the full understanding of this marvelous example was not given me in that time. ¶ In which misty example the properties of the revelation be yet much hidden. And notwithstanding this I saw and understood that every Showing is full of privities. And therefore I must now needs tell of three properties in which I am somewhat eased. ¶ The first is the beginning of teaching that I understood therein at the same time. ¶ The second is the inward learning that I have understood therein since. ¶ The third is the whole Revelation from the beginning to the end, that is to say of this book, which our Lord God of his goodness brings oftentimes freely to the sight of my understanding. ¶ And these three are so oned as to my understanding that I cannot nor may separate them. And by these three as one I have teaching whereby I ▨▨▨ ought to believe and trust in our Lord God, who of the same goodness that he showed it and for the same end, right so of the same goodness and for the same end he shall declare it to us when it is his will. ¶ For (S) fifteen (Ρ) twenty (SΡ) years after the time of the Showing save three months I had teaching inwardly, as I shall say. ¶ "It belongs to you to take heed of all the properties and condition that were showed in the example although you think that they be misty and indifferent to your sight." ¶ I assented willingly, with great desire and inwardly with advisement, all the points and properties that were showed in the same time, as much as my wit and understanding would serve. Beginning my beholding at the Lord and at the servant. ¶ And the manner of sitting of the Lord and the place that he sat on, and the colour of his clothing, and the manner of shape, and his cheer without, and his nobleness and his goodness within. ¶ At the manner of standing of the servant. And the place, where and how, at his manner of clothing, the colour and the shape, at his outward behaving and at his inward goodness, and his unloathsomeness. ¶ The Lord who sat solemnly in rest and in peace, I understand that he is God. ¶ The servant who stood before the Lord, I understood that it was showed for Adam, that is to say one man was showed, that time, and his falling to make thereby understanding how God beholds a man and his falling. For in the sight of God all man is one man and one man is all man. ¶ This man was hurt in his might and made most feeble, and he was stunned in his understanding, for he was turned from the beholding of his Lord, but his will was kept whole in God's sight. For his will I saw our Lord commend and approve. But himself was blocked and blinded of the knowing of this will. And this is to him great sorrow and grievous disease. For neither he sees clearly his loving Lord, who is to him full meek and mild, nor does he see truly what himself is in the sight of his loving Lord. And well I know when these two are wisely and truly seen we shall get rest and peace here, in part, and the fullness of the bliss of heaven, by his plenteous grace. ¶ And this was a beginning of teaching which I saw in the same time whereby I might come to knowing in what manner he beholds us in our sin. ¶ And then I saw that only pains blame and punish. And our courteous Lord comforts and sorrows and succours the soul and ever he is to the soul in glad cheer loving and longing to bring us to bliss. ¶ The place where our Lord sat on was simply on the earth, barren and desert, alone in a wilderness, his clothing was wide and broad, and full seemly as becomes a Lord. ¶ The colour of his cloth was blue as azure, most sad and fair, his cheer was merciful. ¶ The colour of his face was fair brown with fulsomely features, his eyes were black, most fair and seemly, showing full of lovely pity and within him a ▨▨▨ height, length, and breadth all full of endless heavens. ¶ And the lovely looking that he looked upon his servant continually, and namely in his falling, I thought it might melt our hearts for love, and burst them in two for joy. The fair looking showed of a seemly mixture which was marvelous to behold. ¶ That one was ruth and pity. ¶ That other was joy and bliss. The joy and bliss pass as far ruth and pity as heaven is above earth. The pity was earthly and the bliss was heavenly. ¶ The ruth in the pity of the Father was of the falling of Adam who is his most

65

loved creature. The joy and the bliss was of his dearworthy Son, who is even with the Father. ¶ The merciful beholding of his lovely cheer fulfilled all earth and descended down with Adam into Hell, with which continuing pity, Adam was kept from endless death. And this mercy and pity dwells with mankind into the time we come up into heaven. ¶ But man is blinded in this life, and therefore we may not see our Father God, as he is. And what time that he of his goodness will show him to man, he shows him homely as man. ¶ Notwithstanding I did not see truly, we ought to know and believe that the Father is not man. ¶ But his sitting on the earth barren and desert means this. ¶ He made man's soul to be his own city, and his dwelling place, which is most pleasing to him of all his works, and what time that man was fallen into sorrow and pain, he was not all seemly to serve of that noble office. And therefore our natural Father would ordain for him no other place, but to sit upon the earth awaiting mankind, who is meddled of earth, till that time by his grace, his dearworthy Son had bought again his city into the noble fairness with his hard travail. ¶ The blueness of the clothing means his steadfastness, the brownness of his fair face with the seemly blackness of the eyes was most according to show his holy solemnity. ¶ The largeness of his clothing which were fair gathered about means he has beclosed in him all heavens and all joy and bliss. ¶ And this was showed in a touch, where I say my understanding was led into the Lord. In which I saw him highly enjoy, for the worshipful restoring that he will and shall bring his servant to, by his plenteous grace. And yet I marveled beholding the Lord and the servant beforesaid. I saw the Lord sit solemnly and the servant standing reverently before his Lord. In which Servant is double understanding. ¶ One without, another within. Outwardly he was clad simply as a labourer, who was ready to work, and he stood full near the Lord, not even before him, but in part to one side, and that on the left. His ▨▨▨▨ clothing was a single white kirtle, old and all defaced, dyed with the sweat of his body, tight fitting to him, and short, as it were a handful beneath the knee, seeming bare, as it should soon be worn out, ready to be ragged and rent. ¶ And in this I marveled greatly, thinking, this is now an unseemly garb for the servant who is so highly loved to stand in, before so worthy a Lord. ¶ And inward in him was showed a ground of love, which love he had to the Lord, was even like to the love the Lord had to him. The wisdom of the servant saw inwardly that there was one thing to do, which should be to the worship of the Lord. ¶ And the servant for love having no regard to himself, nor to anything that might befall him, hastily he

66

started and ran at the sending of his Lord to do that thing which was his will and his worship. For it seemed by his outward clothing that he had been a continual worker and a hard labourer for a long time. ¶ And by the inward sight that I had, both in the Lord and in the servant, it seemed that he was an apprentice. That is to say, newly beginning to work. Which servant was never sent out before. There was a treasure in the earth which the Lord loved. I marveled and thought, what might it be? ¶ And I was answered in my understanding, it is a meat which is lovesome and pleasing to the Lord. For I saw the Lord sitting as a man, and I saw neither meat nor drink wherewith to serve him. This was one marvel. Another marvel was that this solemn Lord had no servant but one. And him he sent out. I beheld thinking what manner labour it might be that the servant should do? And then I understood that he should do the greatest labour and hardest work that is. ¶ He should be a Gardener, digging and ditching, toiling and sweating, and turn the earth upside down, and seek the deepness, and water the plants in time. And in this he should continue his labour, and make sweet floods to run, and noble and plenteous fruits to spring forth which he should bring before the Lord and serve him therewith to his liking. And he should never turn again till he had prepared this meat all ready as he knew the Lord liked it. And then he should take this meat with the drink in the meat and bear it full worshipfully before the Lord. And all this time the Lord should sit on the same place abiding his servant whom he sent out. ¶ And yet I marveled from where the servant came. For I saw in the Lord that he has within himself endless life and all manner of goodness, save that treasure that was in the earth, and that was grounded in the Lord in marvelous deepness of endless love. But it was not all to the worship till this servant had served it thus nobly, and brought it before him, presenting it himself. And around the Lord was nought but wilderness. And I did not understand all that this Parable meant, and therefore I marveled from where the servant came. ¶ In the servant is comprehended the second Person in the Trinity. And in the servant is comprehended Adam, that is to say, all men. ¶ And therefore, when I say the Son, it means the Godhead, who is even with the Father. And where I say the servant it means Christ's manhood, who is rightful Adam. By the nearness of the servant is understood the Son. And by the standing on the left side, is understood Adam. The Lord is the Father God, the servant is the Son Christ Jesus, the holy Ghost is even love which is in them both. ¶ When Adam fell, God's Son fell, from the rightful oneing which was made in heaven. God's Son

67

might not go from Adam, for by Adam I understand all man. Adam fell from life to death into the hollow of this wretched world. And after that into Hell. God's Son fell with Adam into the slade of the Maiden's womb. Who was the fairest daughter of Adam. And that for to excuse Adam from blame in heaven and in earth. And mightily he fetched him out of Hell. ¶ By the wisdom and goodness that was in the servant is understood God's Son. By the poor clothing as a labourer standing near the left side, is understood the manhood and Adam with all the mischief and feebleness that follow. For in all this our good Lord showed his own Son and Adam as but one man. ¶ The virtue and the goodness that we have is of Jesus Christ, the feebleness and the blindness that we have is of Adam. Which two were showed in the servant. And thus has our good Lord Jesus taken upon him all our blame. ¶ And therefore our Father may not nor will no more blame assign to us than to his own Son dearworthy Christ. ¶ Thus was he, the servant, before his coming upon earth standing ready before the Father, on purpose till what time he would send him to do that worshipful deed, by which mankind was brought again into heaven. That is to say, notwithstanding that he is God even with the Father as regarding the Godhead. But in his foreseeing purpose, that he would be man to save man in fulfilling of his Father's will. So he stood before his Father as a servant wilfully taking upon him all our ░ charge. And then he started full readily at the Father's will and immediately he fell full low into the Maiden's womb, having no regard to himself nor to his hard pains. ¶ The white kirtle is his flesh, the singleness of it, that there was right nought between the Godhead and the manhood, the narrowness is poverty, the age is of Adam's wearing, the defacing of sweat of Adam's work, the shortness shows the servant's labour. ¶ And thus I saw the Son standing, saying in his meaning, "Lo, my dear Father, I stand before you in Adam's kirtle, all ready to start and to run. I would be on earth to do your worship when it is your will to send me. How long shall I desire?" ¶ Full truly the Son knows when it was the Father's will. And how long he shall desire. That is to say regarding the Godhead. For he is the wisdom of the Father. Wherefore this meaning was showed in understanding of the manhood of Christ. For all mankind that shall be saved by the sweet Incarnation and blissful Passion of Christ, all is the manhood of Christ. For he is the head. And we be his members. To which members the day and the time is unknown when every passing woe and sorrow shall have an end. And the everlasting joy and bliss shall be fulfilled. Which day and time for to see, all the company of heaven longs. And all that shall be under heaven that shall come there, their way is by longing and desire. Which desire and longing was showed in the servant standing before the Lord or else this in the Son's standing before the Father in Adam's kirtle. For the langour and desire of all mankind that shall be saved appeared in Jesus. For Jesus is all who shall be saved. And all who shall be saved is Jesus, and all of the charity of God, with obedience, meekness, and patience, and virtues that belong to us. ¶ Also in this marvelous Parable I have teaching with me as it were the beginning of an ABC, whereby I may have some understanding of our Lord's meaning. For the privities of the Revelation be hid therein, notwithstanding that all the Showing is full of privities. ¶ The sitting of the Father betokens his Godhead, that is to say for Showing of rest and peace. For in the Godhead may be no labour. And that he showed himself as Lord, means our manhood. ¶ The standing of the servant means travail. To one side and to the left means that he was not all worthy to stand ever right before the Lord. His starting was the Godhead, and the running was the manhood. ¶ For the Godhead starts from the Father into the Maiden's womb, falling into the taking of our nature. And in this falling he took great sore. The sore that he took was our flesh, in which he had also sudden feeling of deadly pains. ¶ By that he stood full of dread before the 🔲 69 Lord, and not even to his right, means that his clothing was not honest to stand even right before the Lord, nor that might not nor should not be his office while he was a labourer. Nor also might he sit in rest and peace with the Lord, till he had won his peace rightfully with his hard work. ¶ And by the left side, that the Father left his own Son wilfully in the manhood to suffer all man's pains without sparing of him. By his kirtle being at the point to be rent into rags, is understood the whips and the scourges, the thorns and the nails, the drawing and the dragging of his tender flesh rending, as I saw, in some part the flesh being rent from the headpan falling into pieces until the time the bleeding failed. And then it began to dry again, clinging to the bone. ¶ And by the wallowing and writhing, groaning and moaning, is understood that he might never rise all mightily from the time that he was fallen into the Maiden's womb, till his body was slain and dead, he yielding the soul into the Father's hands with all mankind for whom he was sent. ¶ And at this point, he began first to show his might, for he went into Hell, and when he was there he raised up the great root out of the deep deepness, which rightfully was knit to him in high heaven. The body was in the grave till Easter Morrow. And from that time he lay never more. ¶ For then was rightfully ended the wallowing and the writhing, the groaning and the moaning. And our foul deadly flesh that God's Son took on him, which was Adam's old kirtle, tight, bare, and short, then by our Saviour was made fair, new, white, and bright, and of endless cleanness, wide and long, fairer and richer, than was then the clothing which I saw on the Father. For that clothing was blue. And Christ's clothing is now of a fair, seemly rainbow, which is so marvelous that I cannot describe it. For it is all of true worship. ¶ Now sits not the Lord on earth in a wilderness, but he sits in his noblest throne which he made in heaven most to his liking. Now stands not the Son before the Father as a servant before the Lord full of dread, humbly clad, in part naked, but he stands before the Father ever right richly clad in blissfull largesse, with a crown upon his head of precious richness. ¶ For it was showed that we be his Crown, which Crown is the Father's joy, the Son's worship, the holy Ghost's liking. And endless marvelous bliss to all who be in heaven. ¶ Now stands not the Son before the Father on the left side as a labourer, but he sits at his Father's right hand in endless rest and peace. But it is not meant that the Son sits on the right hand side beside him as one man sits by another in this life. For there is no such sitting as to my sight in the Trinity. But he sits on his Father's right hand, that is to say, in the highest nobility of the Father's joys. Now is the spouse, God's Son, in peace with his loved wife, who is the fair Maiden of endless joy. Now sits the Son true God and man in his city in rest and peace, which his Father has ordained to him of his endless purpose. And the Father in the Son. And the holy Ghost in the Father and in the Son.

70

❦

(S) God enjoys that he is our Father, Brother, and Spouse. And how the chosen have here a medley of weal and woe, but God is with us in three ways, and how we may eschew sin but never it. (SP) The Fifty-Second Chapter.

And thus I saw that God enjoys that he is our Father, God enjoys that he is our Mother, and God enjoys that he is our true Spouse. And our soul is his loved wife. ¶ And Christ enjoys that he is our brother. And Jesus enjoys that he is our Saviour. ¶ There are five high joys as I understand in which he will that we enjoy, him praising, him thanking, him loving, him endlessly blessing, all who shall be saved. For the time of this life we have in us a marvelous medley both of weal and woe. ¶ We have in us Lord Jesus Uprisen, we have in us the wretchedness and the mischief of Adam's falling dying. By Christ we are steadfastly kept, and by his grace touching we are raised into secure trust of salvation. ¶ And by Adam's Falling we are so broken in our feeling in diverse manner business and by sundry pains, in which we are made dark and so blind that scarcely we can take any comfort. ¶ But in our meaning we abide God, and faithfully trust to have mercy and grace. And this is his own working in us. ¶ And of his goodness he opens the eye of our understanding by which we have sight, sometimes more, and sometimes less. After that God gives the ability to take. And now we are raised into that one, and now we are permitted to fall into that other. ¶ And thus is this medley so marvelous in us that scarce we know of ourself, or of our even-Christian in what way we stand, for the marvelousness of this sundry feeling. ¶ But that same holy assent that we assent to God when we feel him truly, willing to be with him with all our heart, with all our soul, and with all our might. And then we hate and despise our evil stirrings, and all that might be occasion of sin, ghostly and bodily. ¶ And yet nevertheless when this sweetness is hidden, we fall again into blindness and so into woe and tribulation in diverse ways. ¶ But then is this our comfort that we know in our faith, that by the virtue of Christ, who is our keeper, we assent never thereunto, but we grouch there again and endure in pain and woe, praying into the time that he show himself again to us. And thus ⟨⟩ we stand in this medley all the days of our life. But he wills us to trust that he is lastingly with us, and that in three ways. ¶ He is with us in heaven true man in his own Person, us up drawing. And that was showed in the ghostly thirst. And he is with us on earth leading us. And that was showed in the Third Showing, where I saw God in a point. And he is with us in our soul endlessly dwelling, ruling, and guarding us. And that was showed in the Sixteenth Showing, as I shall say. ¶ And thus in the servant was showed the mischief and blindness of Adam's falling. ¶ And in the servant was showed the wisdom and goodness of God's Son. ¶ And in the Lord was showed the ruth and pity of Adam's woe. ¶ And in the Lord was showed the high nobleness and the endless worship that mankind is come to by the virtue of the Passion and the death of his dearworthy Son. And therefore mightily he enjoys in his falling, for the high Rising and fullness of bliss that mankind is come to overpasses what we should have had if he had not fallen. ¶ And thus to see this overpassing nobleness was my understanding led into God in the same time that I saw the servant fallen. ¶ And thus we have now matter of mourning. For our sin is cause of Christ's pains. And we have lastingly matter of joy. For endless love made him to suffer. ¶ And therefore the creature who sees and feels the working of love by grace, hates nought but sin. For of all thing to my sight love and hate are hardest and most unmeasurable contraries. And notwithstanding all this I saw and understood in our Lord's meaning, that we may not in this life keep us from sin, as wholly in full cleanness as we shall be in heaven. ¶ But we may well by grace keep us from the sins which will lead us to endless pains, as holy Church teaches us. And eschew venial sin reasonably with our might. And if we by our blindness and our wretchedness any time fall, that we readily rise, knowing the sweet touching of grace and wilfully amend us, upon the teaching of holy Church, after that the sin is grievous, and go forth to God in love. And neither on the one side fall over low inclining to despair, nor on that other side be over reckless as if we gave no force, but nakedly knowing our feebleness, understanding that we may not stand a twinkling of an eye but by keeping of grace. And reverently cleave to God trusting on him only. ¶ For otherwise is the beholding of God, and otherwise is the beholding of man. For it belongs to man meekly to accuse himself. And it belongs to the proper goodness of our Lord God courteously to excuse man. ¶ And these be two parties that were showed in the double cheer, in which the Lord beheld the falling of his loved servant. ⬚⬚ ¶ That one was showed outwardly, most meekly and mildly, with great ruth and pity. ¶ And that other of inward endless love. ¶ And right thus will our Lord that we accuse ourself wilfully and truly seeing and knowing our falling and all the harms that come thereof, seeing and understanding that we may never restore it, and therewith that we wilfully and truly see and know his everlasting love that he has for us and his plenteous mercy. ¶ And thus graciously to see and know both together is the meek accusing that our Lord asks of us. And himself works it, then it is. And this is the lower part of man's life. ¶ And it was showed in the outward cheer. In which Showing I saw two parts: ¶ That one is the rueful falling of man; ¶ That other is the worshipful Assize that our Lord has made for man. The other cheer was showed inwardly, and that was more highly and all one. ¶ For the life and the virtue that we have in the lower part is of the higher and it comes down to us of the natural love of the self by grace. Between that one and that other is right nought, for it is all one love. Which one blessed love has now in us a double working. For in the lower part are pains and passions, ruths and pities, mercies and forgiveness, and such other that are profitable. ¶ But in the higher part are none of these. But all one high love, and marvelous joy. In which marvelous joy all pains be wholly destroyed. And in this our good Lord showed not only our excusing, but also the worshipful nobleness that he shall bring us to, turning all our blame into endless worship.

(S) The kindness of God assigns no blame to his chosen. For in these is a goodly will that never consents to sin. For the ruthfulness of God must so be knit to these, that there be a substance kept that may never be separated from him. (Sp) The Fifty-Third Chapter.

And I saw that he will we know he takes not harder the falling of any creature who shall be saved, than he took the falling of Adam, whom we know was endlessly loved and securely kept in the time of all his need. And now is blissfully restored in high overpassing joys. For our lord God is so good, so gentle, and so courteous, that he may never assign fault, in whom he shall ever be blessed and praised. ¶ And in this that I have now said was my desire in part answered and my great awe somewhat eased by the lovely gracious Showing of our good Lord. ¶ In which Showing I saw and understood full securely that in every soul that shall be saved is a godly will that never assents to sin nor ever shall. Which will is so good that it may never will ill, but evermore continually it wills good and works good in the sight of God. ¶ Therefore our Lord will we know it with faith and the belief. And namely and truly, that we have all this blessed will whole and safe in our Lord Jesus Christ. For that same nature that heaven shall be fulfilled with needs of God's righteousness so to be knit and oned to him, that therein were kept a substance which might never nor should be parted from him. And that through his own good will in his endless foreseeing purpose. And notwithstanding this rightful knitting and this endless oneing, yet the redemption and the again-buying of mankind is needful and helpful in everything, as it is done for the same intent and to the same end, that holy Church in our faith teaches us. ¶ For I saw that God began never to love mankind, for right the same that mankind shall be in endless bliss fulfilling the joy of God as regards his works, right so the same mankind has been in the foresight of

73

God known and loved from without beginning in his rightful intent. And by the endless assent of the full accord of all the Trinity. The middle Person would be ground and head of this fair nature, out of whom we be all come, in whom we be all enclosed, into whom we shall all go, in him finding our full heaven in everlasting joy by the foreseeing purpose of all the blessed Trinity from without beginning. For before that he made us he loved us. And when we were made we loved him. ¶ And this is a love made of this natural substantial goodness of the holy Ghost, mighty in reason of the might of the Father, and wise in mind of the wisdom of the Son. And thus is man's soul made of God, and in the same point knit to God. And thus I understand that man's soul is made of nought, that is to say, it is made but of nought that is made, as thus: when God should make man's body, he took the clay of earth, which is a matter mixed and gathered from all bodily things, and thereof he made man's body. ¶ But to the making of man's soul he would take right nought, but made it. And thus is the nature made rightfuly oned to the Maker, who is substantial nature unmade, that is God. ¶ And therefore it is that there may nor shall be right nought between God and man's soul. And in the endless love man's soul is kept whole, as the matter of the Revelation means and shows, in which endless love we be led and kept of God and never shall be lost. For he will we know that our soul is a life, which life of his goodness and his grace shall last in heaven without end, him loving, him thanking, him praising. ¶ And right the same we shall be without end, the same we were treasured in God, and hid, known, and loved from without beginning. Wherefore he will we know that the noblest thing that ever he made is mankind, and the fullest substance, and the highest virtue is the blessed soul of Christ. And furthermore he will we know that his dear-

74   worthy soul was preciously knit to him in the making, which knot is subtle, and so mighty that it is oned into God. In which oneing it is made endlessly holy. ¶ Furthermore he will we know that all the souls who shall be saved in heaven without end are knit and oned in this oneing, and made holy in this holiness.

(S) We ought to enjoy that God dwells in our soul and our soul in God, so that between God and our soul is nothing, but as it were all God.

And how faith is ground of all virtue in our soul by the holy Ghost. (Sp) The Fifty-Fourth Chapter. (WSP)

And for the great endless love that God has to all mankind, he makes no separation in love between the blessed soul of Christ and the least soul that shall be saved. For it is full easy to believe and to trust, that the dwelling of the blessed soul of Christ is full high in the glorious Godhead. ¶ And truly as I understand in our Lord's meaning, where the blessed soul of Christ is, there is the substance of all the souls who shall be saved by Christ. (WSPM) ¶ Highly ought we to enjoy that God dwells in our soul, and much more highly ought we enjoy that our soul dwells in God. Our soul is made to be God's dwelling place, and the dwelling place of our soul is God who is unmade. ¶ A high understanding it is inwardly to see and to know that God who is our maker dwells in our soul. And a higher understanding it is inwardly to see and to know our soul that is made dwells in God's substance, of which substance by God, we are who we are. ¶ And I saw no difference between God and our substance but as it were all God. And yet my understanding took that our substance is in God, that is to say that God is God, and our substance is a creature in God. ¶ For the almighty truth of the Trinity is our Father. For he made us and keeps us in him. And the deep wisdom of the Trinity is our Mother, in whom we are all enclosed. The high goodness of the Trinity is our Lord, and in him we are enclosed and he in us. We are enclosed in the Father. And we are enclosed in the Son. And we are enclosed in the holy Ghost. And the Father is enclosed in us, and the Son is enclosed in us, and the holy Ghost is enclosed in us. All Mightiness, All Wisdom, All Goodness, one God, one Lord. ¶ And our faith is a virtue that comes of our natural substance into our sensual soul by the holy Ghost. ¶ In which all our virtues come to us, for without that no man may receive virtue. For it is not else but a right understanding with true belief and secure trust of our being 〔〕 that we are in God, and God in us, which we see not. ¶ And this virtue with all others that God has ordained to us coming therein, works in us great things. For Christ's merciful working is in us, and we graciously accord to him through the gifts and the virtues of the holy Ghost. This working makes us Christ's Children and Christian in living.

(S) Christ is our way leading and presenting us to the Father and forthwith as the soul is infused in the body mercy and grace work. And how the Second Person took our sensuality to deliver us from double death. (SP) The Fifty-Fifth Chapter.

And thus Christ is our way securely leading us in his laws. And Christ in his body mightily bears us up into heaven. ¶ For I saw that Christ having us all in him, who shall be saved by him, worshipfully presents us to his Father in heaven, which present full thankfully his Father receives, and courteously gives it to his Son Jesus Christ, which gift and working is joy to the Father, and bliss to the Son, and delight to the holy Ghost. ¶ And of all things that belong to us it is most liking to our Lord that we enjoy in this joy, which is in the blissful Trinity of our salvation. ¶ And this was seen in the Ninth Showing, where it speaks more of this matter. And notwithstanding all our feeling woe or weal, God wills we understand and believe that we are more truly in heaven than on earth. ¶ Our faith comes of the natural love of our soul, and of the clear light of our reason, and of the steadfast mind which we have of God in our first making. And what time that our soul is inspired into our body in which we are made sensual. Also often mercy and grace begin to work, having of us cure and keeping, with pity and love. In which working the holy Ghost forms in our faith, hope, that we shall come again up above to our substance into the virtue of Christ increased and fulfilled through the holy Ghost. ¶ Thus I understand that the sensuality is grounded in nature, in mercy, and in grace. Which ground enables us to receive gifts that lead us to endless life. For I saw full surely that our substance is in God. ¶ And also I saw that in our sensuality God is. For the self-same point that our soul is made sensual, in the self-same point is the city of God ordained to him from without beginning. In which see he comes and never shall remove it. For God is never out of the soul, in which he dwells blissfuly without end. ¶ And this was seen in the Sixteenth Showing, where it says the place that Jesus takes in our soul, he shall never remove it. And all the gifts that God may give to creatures, he has given to his Son Jesus for us. Which gifts he dwelling in us has enclosed in him into the time that we be grown and aged, our soul with our body. And our body with our soul, in either of them taking help 🔲 of other until we be brought up into stature as nature works. And then in the ground of nature with working of mercy the holy Ghost graciously inspires into us gifts leading to endless life. ¶ And thus was my understanding led of God to see in him and to understand, to comprehend and to know, that our soul is

76

made a Trinity like to the unmade blissful Trinity, known and loved from without beginning. And in the making oned to the maker as it is before said. ¶ This sight was full sweet and marvelous to behold, peaceable and restful, secure and delectable. And for the worshipful oneing that was thus made of God between the soul and body, it needs must be that mankind shall be restored from double death. Which restoring might never be until the time that the second Person in the Trinity had taken the lower part of mankind, to whom the highest was oned in the first making. ¶ And these two parts were in Christ the higher and the lower, which is but one soul. The higher part was one in peace with God in full joy and bliss, the lower part which is sensuality, suffered for the salvation of mankind. ¶ And these two parts were seen and felt in the Eighth Showing, in which my body was fulfilled of feeling and mind of Christ's Passion and his death. ¶ And furthermore with this was a subtle feeling and privy inward sight of the high part that I was showed in the same time, where I might not for the meanwhile look up into heaven. And that was for that mighty beholding of the inward life, which inward life is that high substance, that precious soul, who is endlessly enjoying in the Godhead.

(S) It is easier to know God than our soul for God is to us nearer than that, and therefore if we will have knowing of it we must seek unto God, and he will we desire to have knowledge of Nature, Mercy, and Grace. (Sp) The Fifty-Sixth Chapter.

And thus (ꟲꟷꟳ) I saw full securely that it is readier to us, and more easy to come to the knowing of God, than to know our own soul. ¶ For our soul is so deep grounded in God and so endlessly treasured that we may not come to the knowing thereof, till we have first knowing of God, who is the maker to whom it is oned. ¶ But notwithstanding, I saw that we have naturally of fullness to desire wisely, and truly to know our own soul. Whereby we are taught to seek it where it is, and that is in God. ¶ And thus by gracious leading of the holy Ghost, we should know them both in one. Whether we be stirred to know God, or our soul, they are both good and true. ¶ God is nearer to us than our own soul, for he is ground in whom our soul stands, and he is the means who keeps the substance and the sensuality together so that

77 they shall never ▨▨ separate. For our soul sits in God in very rest, and
our soul stands in God in true strength. ¶ And our soul is naturally rooted
in God in endless love. (ⓌⓈⓅM) And therefore if we will have knowledge of our soul and communing and dalliance therewith, we must
needs seek into our Lord God in whom it is enclosed. (ⓈⓅ) ¶ And of
this enclosing I saw and understood more in the Sixteenth Showing, as
I shall say. (ⓌⓅ) And as regards our substance it may rightfully be
called our soul, and as regards our (Ⓢ) substance and (ⓌⓈⓅ) sensuality, it may rightly be called our soul and that is by the oneing that it has
in God. (ⓌⓈⓅMN) ¶ The worshipful city that our Lord Jesus sits in,
it is our sensuality in which he is enclosed, and our kindly substance is
beclosed in Jesus with the blessed soul of Christ sitting in rest in the
Godhead. ¶ And I saw full surely that it needs must be that we should
be in longing and in penance, into the time that we be led so deep into
God, that we verily and truly know our own soul. And soothly I saw
that into this high deepness, our good Lord himself leads us in the
same love that he made us, and in the same love that he bought us by
mercy and grace through virtue of his blessed Passion. ¶ And notwithstanding all this we may never come to full knowing of God till we first
know clearly our own soul. For until the time that it is in the full strength
we may not be all fully holy, and that is that our sensuality by the
virtue of Christ's Passion be brought up into the substance, with all the
profits of our tribulation that our Lord shall make us to get by mercy
and grace. ¶ I had in part touching, and it is grounded in nature, that is
to say, our reason is grounded in God, who is substantial highness. ¶
Of this substantial nature, mercy and grace spring and spread into us,
working all things in fulfilling of our joy. ¶ These are our grounds in
which we have our being, our increase, and our fulfilling. ¶ For in nature
we have our life and our being. And in mercy and grace we have our
increase and our fulfilling. These be three properties in one goodness,
and where one works all work in the things which now belong to us. ¶
God wills we understand, desiring with all our heart and all our strength
to have knowing of him, more and more, into the time that we be fulfilled. For fully to know them and clearly to see them is nought else but
endless joy and bliss that we shall have in heaven, which God wills
they be begun here in knowing of his love. For only by our reason we
may not profit. But if there we have truly with mind and love, not only
in our natural ground, that we have in God. We may not be saved but if
we have knowing of the same ground, mercy and grace. ¶ For of these
three working together we receive all our goodness. Of the which the

first are goods of nature. For in our first making God gave us as full goods and also greater goods as we might receive only in our spirit. But his foreseeing purpose in his endless wisdom would that we were double.

(S) In our substance we are full, in our sensuality we fail, which God will restore by Mercy and Grace. And how our Nature, which is the higher part, is knit to God in the making, and God Jesus is knit to our nature in the lower part in our flesh taking. And of Faith spring other virtues. And Mary is our Mother. (Sp) The Fifty-Seventh Chapter.

And as regards our substance he made us noble and so rich that ever more we work his will and his worship. Where I say "we," it means "man who shall be saved." ¶ For truly I saw that we are whom he loves, and do what he likes lastingly without any stopping. And of the great riches and of the high noble virtues by measure come to our soul, what time it is knit to our body, in which knitting we are made sensual. ¶ And thus in our substance we are full. And in our sensuality we fail. Which failing God will restore and fulfill by working of mercy and grace, plenteously flowing into us of his own natural goodness, and thus his natural Godhead goodness makes that mercy and grace work in us, and the natural Godhead that we have of him enables us to receive the working of mercy and grace. I saw that our nature is in God whole in which he makes diverse satisfactions flowing out of him to work his will, whose nature keeps, and mercy and grace restore and fulfill. ¶ And of these none shall perish. For our nature which is the higher part, is knit to God in the making, and God is knit to our nature, which is the lower part of our flesh taking. ¶ And thus in Christ our two natures are oned. For the Trinity is comprehended in Christ in whom our higher part is grounded and rooted, and our lower part the second Person has taken, which nature first to him was ordained. ¶ For I saw full securely that all the works that God has done or ever shall were fully known to him and seen before from without beginning. And for love he made mankind and for the same love, himself would be man. ¶ The next good that we receive is our faith in which our profiting begins, and it comes of the high riches of our natural substance, into our sensual soul. And it is grounded in us and we in that through the natural goodness of God by the working of mercy and grace, and thereof come all other goods by which we are led and saved. For the Commandments of God come therein. In which we ought to have two kinds of understanding. (ÞN) ¶ That one is we owe to understand and know (SÞN) which are his bidding, to love and to keep them. ¶ That other is that we ought to know his forbiddings, to hate and to refuse them. For in these two is all our working comprehended. Also in our faith come the seven Sacraments, each following the other in order as God has ordained them to us, and all manner of virtues. For the same virtues that we have received of our substance, given to us in nature by the goodness of God, the same virtues, by the working of mercy, are given to us in grace through the holy Ghost renewed, which virtues and gifts are treasured to us in Jesus Christ. (SÞ) ¶ For in that same time that God knitted him to our body in the Maiden's womb, he took our sensual soul, in which taking, he having us all enclosed in him, he oned it to our substance. In which oneing he was perfect man. For Christ having knit in him each man who shall be saved is perfect man. ¶ Thus our Lady is our Mother in whom we are all enclosed, and of her born in Christ, for she who is Mother of our Saviour is mother of all who shall be saved in our Saviour. And our Saviour is our very Mother, in whom we be endlessly born and never shall come out of him. Plenteously and fully and sweetly was this showed. And it is spoken of in the First Showing, where he says we are all enclosed in him and he is enclosed in us. ¶ And that is spoken of in the Sixteenth Showing where it says he sits in our soul. For it is his liking to reign in our understanding blissfully and sit in our soul restfully, and to dwell in our soul endlessly, us all working into him. In which working he will we be his helpers giving to him all our attention, learning his lore, keeping his laws, desiring that all be done that he does, truly trusting in him. For soothly I saw that our substance is in God.

(S) God was never displeased with his chosen wife, and of three properties in the Trinity, Fatherhood, Motherhood, and Lordship, and how our substance is in every Person, but our sensuality is in Christ alone. (SÞ) The Fifty-Eighth Chapter.

Ｇod the blissful Trinity who is ever lasting and being, right as he is endless from without beginning, right so it was in his endless purpose to make mankind. Which fair nature first ordained to his own Son, the second Person. And when he would, by full accord of all the Trinity, he made us all at once. ¶ And in our making he knit us and oned us to himself. By which oneing we are kept as clean and as noble as we were made. By the virtue of that same precious oneing. We love our Maker, and like him, praise him, and thank him and endlessly enjoy in him. ¶ And this is the work which is wrought continually in every soul who shall be saved, which is the godly will beforesaid. ¶ And thus in our making God Almighty is our natural Father, and God All Wisdom is our natural Mother, with the love and the goodness of the holy Ghost, ▨ which is all one God, one Lord. And in the knitting and in the oneing he is our very true spouse. And we his loved wife and his fair maiden, with which wife he is never displeased. For he says "I love you and you love me, and our love shall never be parted in two." I beheld the working of all the blessed Trinity in which beholding I saw and understood these three properties, the property of the Fatherhood, the property of the Motherhood, and the property of the Lordship in one God. In our Father Almighty we have our keeping and our bliss, as regards our natural substance, which is to us by our making from without beginning. And in the second Person, in wit and wisdom we have our keeping, as regards our sensuality, our restoring and our saving. For he is our Mother, Brother, and Saviour. And in our good Lord the holy Ghost we have our rewarding and our yielding, for our living and our travail, and endless overpassing all that we desire in his marvelous courtesy of his high plenteous grace. For all our life is in three. ¶ In the first we have our being. ¶ And in the second we have our increasing. ¶ And in the third we have our fulfilling. ¶ The first is nature. ¶ The second is mercy. ¶ The third is grace. ¶ For the first, I saw and understood that the high might of the Trinity is our Father. And the deep wisdom of the Trinity is our Mother. And the great love of the Trinity is our Lord. And all this we have in nature and in our substantial making. And furthermore I saw that the second Person who is our substantial Mother, that same dearworthy Person is (ꝑ) now (Ѕꝑ) become our sensual Mother. For we are double of God's making, that is to say, substantial and sensual. Our substance is the higher part, which we have in our Father God Almighty. ¶ And the second Person of the Trinity is our Mother in nature in our substantial making, in whom we are grounded and rooted. And he is our Mother in mercy in our sensuality taking flesh. And thus our Mother is working to us in diverse ways in whom our parts are kept undivided. For in our Mother Christ we profit and increase. And in mercy he reforms us and restores. ¶ And, by the virtue of his Passion and his death and Uprising ones us to our substance. ¶ Thus works our Mother in mercy to all his children who are to him humble and obedient. And grace works with mercy and namely in two properties, as it was showed. Which work belongs to the third Person, the holy Ghost. He works, rewarding and giving. Rewarding is a large giving of truth that the Lord does to him who has travailed. ¶ And giving is a courteous working which he does freely of grace fulfilling and overpassing all that is deserved of creatures. ¶ Thus in our Father God Almighty we have our being. And in our Mother of mercy we have our reforming and restoring in whom our parts are oned, and all made perfect man. And by yielding and giving in grace of the holy Ghost we are fulfilled. And our substance is our Father God Almighty. And our substance is our Mother God All Wisdom. And our substance is in our Lord the holy Ghost, God, all goodness. For our substance is whole in each Person of the Trinity, who is one God. ¶ And our sensuality is only in the second Person, Christ Jesus, in whom is the Father and the holy Ghost. And in him and by him we are mightily taken out of Hell and out of the wretchedness on earth and worshipfully brought up into heaven, and blissfully oned to our substance increased in riches and nobleness by all the virtue of Christ, and by the grace and working of the holy Ghost.

❦

(S) Wickedness is turned to bliss by mercy and grace in the chosen. For the property of God is to do good against evil by Jesus our Mother in natural grace, and the highest soul in virtue is meekest, of which ground we have other virtues. (SP) The Fifty-Ninth Chapter.

A nd all this bliss we have by mercy and grace, which manner of bliss we might never have had nor known, but if the properties of the goodness which is God had been contraried, whereby we might have this bliss. For wickedness has been suffered to arise contrary to the goodness. And the goodness of mercy and grace contraried against the wickedness and turned all to goodness and to worship to all these who shall be saved. For it is the property in God which does good against evil. ¶ Thus, Jesus Christ who does good against evil is our true Mother. We have our being of him where the ground of Motherhood begins with all the sweet keeping of love that endlessly follows. ¶ As truly as God is our Father, as truly God is our Mother, and that showed he in all, and namely in these sweet words where he says, "I it am," that is to say, "I it am, the might and the goodness of the Fatherhood, I it am, the wisdom and the nature of the Motherhood, I it am, the light and the grace that is all blessed love, I it am, the Trinity, I it am, the Unity. I am the sovereign goodness of all manner of things. I am who makes you to love, I am who makes you to long, I it am, the endless fulfilling of all true desires." ¶ For then the soul is highest, noblest, and worthiest, when yet it is lowest, meekest, and mildest. ¶ And of this substantial ground we have all our virtues, and our sensuality by gift of nature and by helping and aiding of mercy and grace, without which we may not profit. ▨▨▨ (Sp) ¶ Our high Father God Almighty who is being, he knew us and loved us from before any time. Of which knowing in his marvelous deep charity by the foreseeing endless counsel of all the blessed Trinity he would that the second Person should become our Mother, our Brother, and our Saviour. ¶ Whereof it follows that as truly as God is our Father, as truly God is our Mother. Our Father wills, our Mother works, our good Lord the holy Ghost confirms. ¶ And therefore it belongs to us to love our God in whom we have our being, him reverently thanking and praising of our making, mightily praying to our Mother of mercy and pity. And to our Lord, the holy Ghost, of help and grace. ¶ For in these three is all our life, Nature, Mercy, and Grace. Whereof we have meekness, mildness, patience, and pity, and hating of sin and wickedness. For it belongs properly to virtues to hate sin and wickedness. ¶ And thus is Jesus our true Mother in nature of our first making. ¶ And he is our true Mother in grace, by taking of our created nature. All the fair working and all the sweet natural offices of dearworthy Motherhood are proper to the second Person, for in him we have this godly will, whole and saved without end, both in nature and in grace of his own proper goodness. ¶ I understood three kinds of beholding of Motherhood in God. The first is ground of our nature making. ¶ The second is taken of our nature, and there begins the Motherhood of grace. ¶ The third is Motherhood of working. And therein is a forthspreading by the same grace, of length, and breadth, and of height, and of deepness without end and all is his own love.

❦

(S) How we be bought again and forth spread by mercy and grace of our sweet, kind, and ever loving Mother Jesus, and of the properties of Motherhood. But Jesus is our true Mother, not feeding us with milk but with himself opening his side on to us and challenging all our love. (SP) The Sixtieth Chapter. (WSP)

But now I must say a little more of this forth spreading, as I understand in the meaning of our Lord, how that we be brought again by the Motherhood of mercy and grace into our natural stead, where we were made by the Motherhood of natural love, which natural love never leaves us. ¶ Our natural Mother, our gracious Mother. For he would all wholly become our Mother in all thing. He took the ground of his work full low, and full mildly in the Maiden's womb, taking flesh of her. And that he showed in the First Showing when he brought that meek Maiden before the eye of my understanding in the simple stature as she was when she conceived. That is to say our high God is sovereign wisdom of all. In this low place 〔꒐꒦꒐〕 he went and prepared himself all ready in our poor flesh, himself to do the service and the office of Motherhead in all thing. ¶ The Mother's service is nearest, readiest, and securest. Nearest for it is most of nature, readiest for it is most of love, and securest for it is most of truth. This office might not, nor could ever be done to the full but by (W) Christ (WSP) Jesus, God and man, him alone. We know that all our mothers bear us is to pain and to dying. And what is that? But our true Mother Jesus, he all love, bears us to joy and to endless living, blessed must he be. Thus he sustains us within himself in love and travailed into the full time, that he would suffer the sharpest throes, and the most grievous pains that ever were, or ever shall be, and died at the last. And when he had done and so born us to bliss, yet might not all this make amends of his marvelous love. And that showed he in these high overpassing words of love, "If I might suffer more I would suffer more." He might no more die but he would not stop from working. Wherefore he needs to feed us for the dearworthy love of Motherhood has made him debtor to us. ¶ The Mother may give her Child to suck of her milk, but our precious Mother Jesus, he may feed us with himself. And does most courteously and most tenderly with the blessed Sacrament (W) of his body and blood, (WSP) that is precious food of very life and with all the sweet sacraments he sustains us most mercifully and graciously. And so meant he in this blessed word where he said, "I it am whom holy Church preaches to you and teaches you, that is to say all the health and life of the Sacraments, all the virtue and grace of my word, all that goodness that is ordained in holy Church for you, I it am." The Mother may lay the Child tenderly to her breast, but our tender (𝔚) Lord (𝔖𝔭) Mother (𝔚𝔖𝔭) Jesus, he may homely lead us into his blessed breast by his sweet open side and show us therein part of the Godhead and the joys of heaven with ghostly secureness of endless bliss. ¶ And that he showed in the Ninth Showing, giving the same understanding in this sweet word where he says, "Lo, how I love you," beholding into his blessed side, enjoying. This fair lovely word, "Mother," it is so sweet and so natural of the self, that it may not truly be said of none, nor to none, but of him and to her who is true Mother of him and of all. ¶ To the property of Motherhood belongs natural love, wisdom, and knowing, and it is good. For though it be so that our bodily forthbringing be but little, low, and simple in regard to our ghostly forthbringing, yet it is he who does it in the creatures by whom it is done. ¶ The natural loving Mother who understands and knows the need of her child she keeps it full tenderly as the nature and the condition of Motherhood will. And as it grows in age, she changes her working but not her love. And when it is grown of more age she suffers that it be bruised in breaking down of vices to make the child receive virtues and graces. ¶ This working with all that be fair and good, our Lord does it in them by whom it is done. Thus he is our Mother in nature by the working of grace in us in the lower part for love of the higher part. ¶ And he will that we know it, for he will have all our love fastened to him. And in this I saw that all our debt that we owe by God's bidding, by Fatherhood and Motherhood, for God's Fatherhood and Motherhood is fulfilled in true loving of God which blessed love Christ works in us. ¶ And this was showed in all, and namely in the high plenteous words where he says, "I it am whom you love."

84

(𝔖) Jesus uses more tenderness in our ghostly bringing forth, though he suffers us to fall in knowing of our wretchedness. He hastily raises us, not breaking his love for our trespass, for he may not suffer his child to perish. For he will that we have the property of a child fleeing to him always in our need. (𝔖𝔭) The Sixty-First Chapter. (𝔚𝔖𝔭)

H nd in our ghostly forthbringing he uses more tenderness of keeping, without any likeness. By as much as our soul is of more price in his sight, he kindles our understanding, he directs our ways, he eases our conscience, he comforts our soul, he lightens our heart, and gives us in part knowing and loving in his blissful Godhead, with gracious mind in his sweet manhood and his blessed Passion, with courteous marveling in his high overpassing goodness. And makes us to love all that he loves for his love, and be paid with him with all that he does and in and all his works. ¶ And when we fall, hastily he raises us by his lovely calling and gracious touching. And when we be thus strengthened by his sweet working then we wilfully chose him by his sweet grace, to be his servants and his lovers lastingly without end. ¶ And yet after this he suffers some of us to fall harder and more grievously than ever we did before as we think. And then believe we that be not all wise that all were nought that we have begun. But it is not so. For we need to fall, and we need to see it. For if we fell not, we should not know how feeble and how wretched we are of our self, nor also we should not so fulsomely know the marvelous love of our Maker. For we shall truly see in heaven without end that we have grievously sinned in this life. ¶ And notwithstanding this we shall see that we were 🔶 never hurt in his love, nor were ever the less of price in his sight. And by the testing of this falling we shall have a high marvelous knowing of love in God without end. For hard and marvelous is that love which may not nor will not be broken for trespass. And this is one understanding of profit. ¶ Another is the lowness and meekness that we shall get by the sight of our falling, for thereby we shall highly be raised in heaven, to which rising we might never have come without that meekness. And therefore we need to see it, and if we see it not, though we fell, it should not profit us. And commonly first we fall and then we see it, and both is of the mercy of God. ¶ The Mother may suffer the child to fall sometimes and be discomforted in diverse ways for its own profit. But she may never suffer that any manner of peril come to the Child for love. ¶ And though our earthly mother may allow her Child to perish, our heavenly Mother Jesus may not suffer us who are his Children to perish. For he is almighty, all wisdom and all love, and so is none but he, Blessed must he be. ¶ But often when our falling, and our wretchedness is showed us, we are so sore adread, and so greatly ashamed of our self, that scarce we know where we may hold us. But then wills not our courteous Mother that we flee away, for him were nothing more loathful. ¶ But he will then that we use the condition of Childhood,

85

for when it is diseased or afraid, it runs hastily to the Mother and if it may do no more it cries on the Mother for help with all its might. So will he that we do as a meek Child, saying thus, "My natural Mother, my gracious Mother, my dearworthy Mother, have mercy on me, I have made myself foul and unlike you, and I neither may nor can amend it, but with your privy help and grace." And if we feel us not then eased soon we be secure that he uses the condition of a wise Mother. For if he sees that it be more profit to us to mourn and to weep, he suffers it with ruth and pity into the best time for love. And he will then that we use the property of a Child who evermore naturally trusts to the love of the Mother in weal and in woe. And he will that we take us mightily to the faith of holy Church, and find there our dearworthy Mother in solace of true understanding with all the blessed Common. ¶ For one singular person may often be broken as it seems to itself, but the whole body of holy Church was never broken nor ever shall be without end. ¶ And therefore a secure thing it is, a good and a gracious to will meekly, and mightily be sustained and oned to our Mother holy Church who is Christ Jesus. For the flood of mercy that is his dearworthy blood and precious water is plenteous to make us fair and clean. The blessed wound of our Saviour be open and enjoy to heal us. ¶ The sweet gracious hands of our Mother be ready and diligent about us. For he in all this working uses the office of a kind nurse and has not else to do but to attend to the salvation of her Child. It is his office to save us, it is his worship to do us, and it is his will we know it. For he will we love him sweetly and trust in him meekly and mightily. And this showed he in these gracious words, "I keep you most securely."

86

(S) The love of God suffers never his chosen to lose time. For all their trouble is turned into endless joy. And how we are all bound to God for nature and for grace. For all nature is in man, and we need not to seek out to know sundry natures but to holy Church. (Sp) The Sixty-Second Chapter.

For in that time he showed our frailty and our fallings, our breakings and our noughtings, our despites and our outcastings and all our woe, so much as I thought it may befall in this life. ¶ And therewith he showed his blessed might, his blessed wisdom, his blessed love that he keeps us in this time, as tenderly and as sweetly to his worship and as surely to our salvation, as he does when we are in most solace and comfort. And thereto he raises us ghostly and highly in heaven, and turns it all to his worship and to our joy without end. For his love allows us never to lose time. And all this is of the natural goodness of God by the working of grace. ¶ God is natural in his being, that is to say, that goodness that is natural, it is God. He is the ground, he is the substance, he is the same thing that is nature. And he is true Father and true Mother of nature. And all natures that he has made to flow out of him to work his will, shall be restored and brought again into him by the salvation of man, through the working of grace. ¶ For of all natures that he has set in diverse creatures in part, in man is all the whole, in fullness and in virtue, in fairness and in goodness, in royalty and in nobility, in all manner of solemnity, of preciousness and worship. ¶ Here may we see that we are all bound to God for nature, and we are all bound to God for grace. Here may we see we need not greatly to seek far out to know sundry natures, but to holy Church into our Mother's breast, that is to say into our own soul where our Lord dwells. And there shall we find all now in faith and in understanding. And after truly in himself clearly in bliss. But no man nor woman take this singularly to himself. For it is not so, it is general, for it is our precious Mother Christ. And to him was this fair nature arranged for the worship and nobleness of man's making, and for the joy and the bliss of man's salvation, right as he saw, understood and knew from without beginning.

87   (S) Sin is more painful than Hell and vile and hurting nature, but grace saves nature and destroys sin. The children of Jesus be not yet all born, who pass not the stature of childhood, living in feebleness until they come to heaven where joys are ever newly beginning, without end. (Sp) The Sixty-Third Chapter.

Here may we see that we have truly of nature to hate sin, and we have truly of grace to hate sin. For nature is all good and fair in the self. And grace was sent out to save nature, and destroy sin, and bring again fair nature to the blessed point from whence it came, that is

God, with more nobility and worship by the virtuous working of grace. ¶ For it shall be seen before God of all his holy ones in joy without end, that nature has been assayed in the fire of tribulation, and therein found no lack nor fault. Thus are nature and grace of one accord, for grace is God as nature is God. He is two in manner of working, and one in love. And neither of them works without the other, none be separated. ¶ And when we by the mercy of God and with his help accord us to nature and grace, we shall see truly that sin is truly viler and more painful than Hell without any likeness. For it is contrary to our fair nature, for as truly as sin is unclean, so truly is it unnatural. ¶ And thus a horrible thing to see to the loved soul, that would be all fair and shining in the sight of God, as nature and grace teach. ¶ But be we not afraid of this, but inasmuch as dread may help us, but meekly make we our moan to our dearworthy Mother and he shall all besprinkle us in his precious blood, and make our soul full soft and full mild, and heal us full fair by process of time, right as it is most worship to him and joy to us without end. ¶ And of this sweet fair working he shall never cease nor stop till all his dearworthy children be born and brought forth. And that showed he where he showed understanding of ghostly thirst, that is the love longing, that shall last till Doomsday. ¶ Thus in our true Mother Jesus our life is grounded in the foreseeing wisdom of himself, from without beginning with the high might of the Father, and the high sovereign goodness of the holy Ghost. And in the taking of our nature he quickened us in his blessed dying upon the Cross, he bare us to endless life. ¶ And from that time and now, and ever shall unto Doomsday, he feeds us and nourishes us. And right as that high sovereign nature of Motherhood wills and as the natural need of Childhood asks. Fair and sweet is our heavenly Mother in the sight of our soul, precious and lovely are the gracious children in the sight of our heavenly Mother with mildness and meekness, and all the fair virtues that belong to Children in nature. ¶ For naturally the Child despairs not of the Mother's love, naturally the Child presumes not of the self, naturally the Child loves the Mother, and each one the other. These are the fair virtues, with all others that be like wherewith ⟨⟩ our heavenly Mother is served and pleased. ¶ And I understood no lower stature in this life than Childhood in feebleness and failing of strength and of intellect, until the time that our gracious Mother has brought us up to our Father's bliss. And than shall it truly be made known to us his meaning in these sweet words where he says, "All shall be well, and you shall see it yourself that all manner of thing shall be well."

(ꝑ) The Fifteenth Revelation. The Sixty-Fourth Chapter. (Sꝑ)

And then shall the bliss of our Mother in Christ be new to begin in the joys of our (ꝑ) Father (Sꝑ) God, which new beginning shall last without end, newly beginning. Thus I understood that all his blessed Children who be come out of him by nature shall be bought again unto him by grace.

(S) The Fifteenth Revelation is as it showed, etc. The absence of God in this life is our full great pain, beside other travail, but we shall suddenly be taken from all pain, having Jesus to our Mother, and our patient abiding is greatly pleasing to God. And God will take our disease lightly for love, thinking us always at the point to be delivered.

The Sixty-Fourth Chapter. (SꝑꜤ) ¶

Before this time I had great longing and desire of God's gift, to be delivered of this world and of this life. (Ꜥ) For I should be with my God in bliss, (ꟲꜤ) where I hope securely, through his mercy, to be without end. (ꟲSꝑꜤ) For often I beheld the woe that is here, and the weal and the bliss that is being there. And if there had been no pain in this life on earth, but the absence of our Lord, I thought it was sometimes more than I might bear. And this made me to mourn and busily to long. ¶ And also of my own wretchedness, sloth and weakness, so that I desired not to live and to work as I had to do. And to all this our courteous Lord answered for comfort and patience and said these words, "Suddenly you shall be taken from all your pain, from all your sickness, from all your disease, and from all your woe, and you shall come up above. And you shall have me to your reward. And you shall be fulfilled of joy and of bliss. And you shall have no manner of pain, (ꟲꝑ) no manner of sickness, (ꟲSꝑꜤ) no manner of misliking, no wanting of will, but ever joy and bliss without end. What should it then grieve you to suffer awhile, since it is my will and my worship." And in this word, "Suddenly you shall be taken," I saw that God rewards man of the patience that he has in abiding God's will and of his time. And that man lengthens his patience over the time of his living. For unknowing of his time of passing. ¶ That is a great profit. For if a man knew his time, he should not have patience over that time. And as God will, while the soul is in the body, it seems to the self, that it is ever at the point to be taken. For all this life and this langour that we have here is but a point. And when we are taken suddenly out of pain into bliss, then pain shall be nought. ¶ And in this time I saw a body lying on the earth, which body showed heavy and ugly without shape and form, as it were, a bloated quagmire of a stinking bog, and suddenly out of this body sprang a full fair creature, a little Child, fully shaped and formed, swift and lively, whiter than a lily, which sharply glided up into heaven. ¶ And the swelling of the body betokens great wretchedness of our deadly flesh, and the littleness of the Child betokens the cleanness of purity in the soul. ¶ And I thought with this body is left no fairness of this Child, nor on this Child dwells any foulness of this body. It is full blissful, man to be taken from pain, more than pain to be taken from man. For if pain be taken from us it may come again. Therefore it is a sovereign comfort and a blissful beholding in a loving soul, if we shall be taken from pain. ¶ For in this promise I saw a marvelous compassion that our Lord has in us for our woe and a courteous promising of clean deliverance. For he will that we be comforted in the overpassing joy. And that he showed in these words, "And you shall come up above, and you shall have me to your reward, and you shall be fulfilled of joy and bliss." It is God's will that we set the point of our thought in this blissful beholding as often as we may, and as long [End ⅦI] time keep us therein with his grace. For this is a blessed contemplation to the soul that is led of God and full greatly to his worship for the time that it lasts. ¶ And we fall again to our heaviness and ghostly blindness and feeling of pains ghostly and bodily by our frailty, it is God's will that we know that he has not forgotten us. And so means he in these words and says for comfort, "And you shall never more have pain, nor manner of sickness, nor manner of misliking, nor wanting of will, but ever joy and bliss without end. What should it then grieve you to suffer a while, seeing it is my will and my worship." It is God's will we take his promises and his comfortings as largely and as mightily as we may take them. And also he will that we take our abiding and our diseases as lightly as we may take them, and set them at nought. For the lighter we take them, and the less price we set at them for love, the less pain shall we have in the feeling of them, and the more thanks and reward shall we have for them.

89

(S) He who chooses God for love with reverent meekness is secure to be saved. Which reverent meekness sees the Lord marvelously great and the self marvelously little. And it is God's will we dread nothing but him, for the power of our enemy is taken in our friend's hand. And therefore all that God does shall be great liking to us. (SP) The Sixty-Fifth Chapter.

And thus I understood (H) In this blessed Revelation I was truly taught that (SPH) what man or woman wilfully chooses God in this life for love, he may be secure that he is (SP) loved without end, which endless love works in him that grace. Keep this truly. For he wills that we keep this trusting that we be all secure in hope of the bliss of heaven while we are here, as we shall be in secureness when we are there. ¶ And ever the more liking and joy that we take in this sureness with reverence and meekness the better he likes it. ¶ As it was showed, this reverence that I mean is a holy courteous dread of our Lord to which meekness is knit, and that is that a creature sees the Lord marvelously great, and the self marvelously little. ¶ For these virtues are had endlessly to the beloved of God, and it must now be seen and felt in measure by the gracious presence of our Lord when it is. ¶ Which presence in all thing is most desired, for it works marvelous secureness in true faith and secure hope by greatness of charity in dread that is sweet and delectable. It is God's will that ⟨⟩ I see my self as much bound to him in love, as if he had done for me all that he has done. ¶ And thus should every soul think in regard of his lover, that is to say, the Charity of God makes in us such a Unity, that, when it is truly seen, no man can part himself from another. (H) For I am secure that if there had been none other but I who should be saved, God would have done all that he has done for me and so should each soul think in knowing of his lover, forgetting if he might all creatures and thinking. (SP) And thus ought our soul to think that God has done for him all that he has done. ¶ And this he shows to make us love him, and nought dread but him. For it is his will that we know that all the might of our enemy is taken into our friend's hand, and therefore the soul who knows this securely, shall not dread but him whom he loves. All our dreads he sets among passions and bodily sickness and imaginations. And therefore though we be in so much pain, woe and disease, that we can think right nought but that we are in or that we feel, as soon as we may, we pass lightly over and we set it at nought. And why? For God wills we know him. For if we know him and love him, reverently dreading him, we shall have peace, and be in great rest. And it shall be great liking to us,

90

all that he does. And this showed our Lord in these words, "What should it then grieve you to suffer a while, since it is my will and my worship." (Ⅎ) And here was an end of all that the Lord showed me that day. (Ƨℙ) ¶ Now I have told you of Fifteen Showings as God vouchsafes to minister them to mind, renewed by lightings and touchings, I hope of the same spirit that showed them all. Of which Fifteen Showings, the first began early in the morning about the hour of four (or ten o'clock, before noon) and it lasted showing by process full fair and securely, each following the other, until it was nine (or three o'clock in the afternoon) of the day, overpassed.

The Sixteenth Revelation, (Ƨ) etc. And it is conclusion and confirmation to all Fifteen Showings. And of her frailty and mourning in disease, and light speaking after the great comfort of Jesus, saying she had raved, which being her great sickness, I suppose was but venial sin. But yet the devil had great power to vex her near to death. (Ƨℙ) The Sixty-Sixth Chapter.

And after this the good Lord showed the Sixteenth Revelation on the night following as I shall say after, which Sixteenth was conclusion and confirmation to all Fifteen Showings. ¶ But first I needs must tell you, regarding my feebleness, wretchedness, and blindness. ¶ I have said in the beginning, "And in this all my pain was suddenly taken from me." Of which pain I had no grief nor disease, as long as the Fifteen Showings lasted following. And at the end all was close. And I saw no more. And soon I felt that I should live and langour. And immediately my sickness came again, first in my head with a sound and a din, and suddenly all my body was fulfilled with sickness like as it was before. (Ⅎ)

{And after this, I fell into my self and into my bodily sickness understanding that I should live. (ƧℙℲ) And I was as barren and as dry as if I never had comfort but little, and as a wretch, I moaned and heaved for feeling of my bodily pains, and for failing of comfort ghostly and bodily, (Ⅎ) and thought it great anguish that I should live longer. (ƧℙℲ) ¶ Then came a monk to me and asked me how I fared, and I said I had raved today, and he laughed out loud and inwardly. ¶ And I said the Cross that stood (Ƨℙ) before my face, (Ⅎ) at my bed's foot, (SP) I thought it bled fast, and with this word, the person I spoke to became all grave and marveled. And immediately I was sore ashamed 91 and astonished for my recklessness. And I thought this man takes seriously the least word that I might say. Then I saw no more thereof. ¶ And when I saw that he took it so sadly and with so great reverence I wept, full greatly ashamed, and would have made my confession, but at that time I could tell it to no priest. For I thought, how should a priest believe me, when by saying "I raved" I showed myself to believe not our Lord God. I believed truly for the time that I saw him, and so was then my will and my meaning ever to do without end, but as a fool, I let it pass from my mind. ¶ Ah, lo, I, a wretch, this was a great sin, a great unnaturalness, that I for folly of feeling a little bodily pain so unwisely lost for the time the comfort of all this blessed Showing of our Lord God. ¶ Here may you see what I am of my self. But herein would our courteous Lord not leave me. And I lay still till night, trusting in his mercy, and then I began to sleep. (P)

The Sixty-Seventh Chapter. (SPH)

And in my sleep at the beginning I thought the fiend set him at my throat thrusting forth a face near mine like a young man, and it was long and wonderfully lean, I never saw none such. The color was red like the tilestone when it is new burnt, with black spots therein, like black freckles fouler than the tile stone. His hair was red as unscored rust, with side locks hanging on the jowls. He grinned on me with a shrewd semblance showing me white teeth, and so much I thought it the more ugly. ¶ Body nor hands had he none shapely, but with his paws he held me in the throat, and would have strangled me, but he might not. This ugly Showing was made sleeping, and so was none other. And in all this time I trusted to be saved and kept by the mercy of God. ¶ And our courteous Lord gave me grace to wake, and scarcely had I my life. ¶ The persons who were with me beheld me and wet my temples, and my heart began to strengthen. And soon a little smoke came in the door with a great heat and a foul stink. ¶ I said, "Benedicite Domine, is it all on fire that is here?" And I believed it had been a bodily fire that should have burnt us all to death. ¶ I asked them who were with me if they felt any stink. They said, "No," they felt none. I said,

"Blessed be God." ¶ For then I knew well it was the fiend, who was come to tempest me. And anon I took to that our Lord has showed me on the same day, with all the faith of holy Church. For I beheld it both as one. And fled thereto as to my comfort. And immediately all vanished away and I was brought to great rest and peace without sickness of body or dread of conscience.

(S) Of the worshipful sight of the soul who is so nobly created, that it might no better have been made, in which the Trinity joys everlastingly. And the soul may have rest in nothing but in God, who sits therein ruling all things. The Sixty-Seventh Chapter. (A)

{B}ut then I was left still awake. (SPA)

And then our Lord opened my ghostly eye and showed me my soul in the midst of my heart. I saw the soul so large as it were an endless world and as it were a blissful kingdom. And by the condition I saw therein I understood, that it is a worshipful city. ¶ In the midst of that city sits our Lord Jesus, God and man, a fair person and of large stature, highest Bishop, solemnest King, worshipfullest Lord. And I saw him clad solemnly, and worshipfully he sits in the soul, even right in peace and rest. And the Godhead rules and guards heaven and earth and all that is. ¶ And the soul is all occupied with the blessed Godhead, who is sovereign might, sovereign wisdom, and sovereign goodness. ¶ The place that Jesus takes in our soul he shall never remove it without end as to my sight. ¶ For in us is his homeliest home and his endless dwelling, and in this he showed the liking that he has of the making of man's soul, (A) and most liking to him to dwell in. (SP) ¶ For as well as the Father might make a creature, and as well as the Son could make a creature, so well would the holy Ghost that man's soul were made, and so it was done. ¶ And therefore the blessed Trinity enjoys without end in the making of man's soul. For he saw from without beginning what should delight him without end. ¶ All thing that he has made shows his Lordship, as understanding was given at the same time, by example of a creature, who is to see great nobleness and kingdoms belonging to a Lord. And when it had seen all the nobleness beneath, there marveling, it was stirred to seek above to the high place where

92

the Lord dwells, knowing by reason that his dwelling is in the worthi-est place. ¶ And thus I understood truly that our soul may never have rest in things that are beneath itself, and when it comes above all crea-tures into the self, yet may it not abide in the beholding of the self. ¶ But all the beholding is blissfully set in God who is the Maker, dwelling therein. For in man's soul is his true home. ¶ And the highest light and the brightest shining of the City is the glorious love of our Lord, as to my sight. ¶ And what may make us more to enjoy in God, than to see in him, that he enjoys highest of all his works. ¶ For I saw in the same Showing that if the blissful Trinity might have made man's soul any better, any fairer, any nobler than it was made, he should not have been fully pleased with the making of man's soul. (𝒫) But for he made man's soul as fair, as good, as precious as he might make it a creature, therefore the blessed Trinity is full pleased without end in the making of man's soul. (Ƨ𝒫) ¶ And he will that our hearts be mightily raised above the deepness of the earth and all vain sorrows, and enjoy in him.

(Ƨ) Of true knowing that it is Jesus who showed all this. And it was no raving. And how we ought to have secure trust in all our tribulation that we shall not be overcome. The Sixty-Eighth Chapter. (Ƨ𝒫Ⱨ)

{ℭhis was a delectable sight and a restful Showing that it is so (Ⱨ) in truth (Ƨ𝒫Ⱨ) without end. And the beholding of this while we are here it is full pleasant to God, and full great speed to us. And the soul who thus beholds it, makes it like to him who is beheld and ones it in rest and peace by his grace. ¶ And this was a singular joy and bliss to me, that I saw him sit. For the secureness of the sitting shows (Ⱨ) to me secureness of his (Ƨ𝒫Ⱨ) endless dwelling. And he gave me knowing truly, that it was he, who showed me all before. And when I had beheld this ▨▨ attentively, then showed (Ⱨ) me (Ƨ𝒫Ⱨ) our good Lord words full meekly without voice, and without opening of lips, right as he had done, and said full sweetly, "Know it well that it was no raving that you saw today, but take it and believe it, and keep you therein, and comfort you therewith, and trust you thereto, and you shall not be overcome." These last words were said for teaching of true secureness, that it is our good Lord who showed me all, right as in the first word that our Lord showed (Ⱨ) me, (Ƨ𝒫Ⱨ) meaning his blessed Passion,

"Herewith is the devil overcome," Right so, he said, in the last word with full true secureness, meaning us all, "You shall not be overcome." And all this teaching in this true comfort, it is general to all my even-Christians as it is said before. And so is God's will. ¶ And these words, "You shall not be overcome," were said full sharply, and full mightily for secureness and comfort against all tribulations that may come. ¶ He said not, "You shall not be tempested, you shall not be travailed, you shall not be diseased," but he said, "You shall not be overcome." God wills that we take heed at these words, and that we be ever mighty in secure trust in weal and woe, for he loves and likes us. And so wills he that we love him and like him, and mightily trust in him. And all shall be well. And soon after all was closed and I saw no more.

(S) Of the second long temptation of the devil to despair. But she mightily trusted to God, and to the faith of holy Church, rehearsing the Passion of Christ by which she was delivered. (P) The Sixty-Ninth Chapter. (SA)

{A}fter this (SPA)

Τhe fiend came again with his heat and with his stink, and made me full busy. The stench was so vile and so painful and bodily heat also dreadful and travailous. Also I heard a bodily jangling and a speech, as it had been of two bodies, and both to my thinking jangled at one time, as if they had held a parliament with a great business and all was soft muttering, as I understood nought of what they said. And all this was to stir me to despair, as I thought, seeming to me as if they scorned bidding of beads which are said boisterously with mouth, failing devout concentration and wise diligence, which we owe to God in our prayers. ¶ And our Lord God gave me grace mightily to trust in him and (A) I trust busily in God (SPA) to comfort my soul with bodily speech as I should have done to another person (A) than myself (SPA) who had been so travailed. I thought that business might not be likened to any bodily business. (P)

The Seventieth Chapter. (ᔑᕟᕼ)

My bodily eye I set in the same cross where I had been in comfort before that time, my tongue (ᕼ) I occupied (ᔑᕟᕼ) with speech of Christ's Passion, and rehearsing the faith of holy Church, and my heart to fasten on God with all the trust and my might (ᕼ) that was in me. (ᔑᕟᕼ) And I thought to my self meaning, ▨▧ "You have now great business to keep yourself in the faith, for you should not be taken of your enemy. Would you now for this time evermore be so busy to keep yourself from sin, this were a good and sovereign occupation." ¶ For I thought truly were I safe from sin, I were fully saved from all the fiends of Hell and enemies of my soul. ¶ And thus he worried me all that night, and on the morn till it was about prime day (dawn). And anon they were all gone and all passed, and then left nothing but stink, and that lasted still awhile. And I scorned him. And thus was I delivered of them by the virtue of Christ's Passion. For therewith is the fiend overcome as our Lord Jesus Christ said before, (ᕼ) to me. Ah, wretched sin. What are you? You are nought. For when I saw that God is all things, I saw you not. And when I saw that God has made all things, I saw you not. And when I saw that God is in all things, I saw you not. And when I saw that God does all things that are done, less and more, I saw you not. And when I saw our Lord Jesus sit in our soul so worshipfully and love and like and rule and govern all that he has made, I saw you not. And thus I am secure that you are nought and all who love you and like you and follow you and wilfully end in you, I am secure they shall be brought to nought with you and endlessly confounded. God shield us all from you. Amen. For charity. And what wretchedness is, I will say as I am taught by the Showing of God. Wretchedness is all thing that is not good, the ghostly blindness that we fall into in the first sin and all that follows of that wretchedness, passions and pains, ghostly or bodily, and all that is on earth or in other places which are not good. And then may be asked of this, "What are we?" And I answer to this, if all were taken from us that is not good, we should be good. When wretchedness is taken from us, God and the soul is all one, and God and man all one. What is all thing on earth that twins us? I answer and say, "In that it serves us, it is good. And in that it shall perish it is wretchedness, and in that a man sets his heart upon it otherwise than thus, it is sin." And for that time that man or woman loves sin, if any be such, he is in pain that passes all pains. And when he loves not sin, but hates it and loves God, all is well. And he who truly does thus, though he sin sometime by frailty or ignorance in his will, he falls not, for he will mightily rise again and behold God, whom he loves in all his will. God has made them to be loved of him or her who has been a sinner. But ever he loves and ever he longs to have our love. And when we mightily and wisely love Jesus, we are in peace.

(S) In all tribulation we ought to be steadfast in the faith, trusting mightily in God. For if our faith had no enmity it should deserve no reward. And how all these Showings are in the faith. The Seventieth Chapter. (SP)

¶ In all this blessed Showing our good Lord gave understanding that the sight should pass. Which blessed Showing the faith keeps with his own good will and his grace. For he left with me neither sign nor token whereby I might know it. ¶ But he left with me his own blessed word in true understanding, bidding me full mightily that I should believe it. And so I do, Blessed must he be. I believe that he is our Saviour who showed it, and that it is the faith that he showed, and therefore I believe it, enjoying. And thereto I am bound by all his own meaning with the next words that follow, "Keep you therein, and comfort you therewith and trust you thereto." Thus I am bound to keep it in my faith. For on the self same day that it was showed, what time that the sight was passed, as a wretch I forsook it and openly I said that I had raved. ¶ Then our Lord Jesus of his mercy would not let it perish, but he showed it all again within in my soul, with more fullness, with the blessed light of his precious love, saying these words full mightily and full meekly, "Know it now well, it was no raving that you saw this day." As if he had said, "Because the sight passed from you, you lost it and could not keep it. But know it now." That is to say, "Now that you see it." This was said not only for the same time but also to set thereupon the ground of my faith, where he said immediately the following, "But take it, **believe** and learn it and keep you therein, and comfort you therewith and trust you thereto, and you shall not be overcome." (P)

The Seventy-First Chapter. (SP)

I n these six words that follow where he says, "Take it," his meaning is to fasten it faithfully in our heart. For he will that it dwell with us in faith to our life's end and after in fullness of joy, willing that we have ever secure faithful trust in his blissful promises, knowing his goodness. For our faith is contraried in divers manners by our own blindness and our ghostly enemy within and without. And therefore our precious lover helps us with ghostly sight and true teaching on sundry manners, within and without, whereby we may know him. ¶ And therefore in what manner he teaches us he will we perceive him wisely, receiving him sweetly, and keeping us in him faithfully. ¶ For above the faith is no goodness kept in this life, as to my sight. And beneath the faith is no help of soul. ¶ But in the faith, there will the Lord that we keep us, for we have by his goodness and his own working to keep us in the faith. And by his suffrance, by ghostly enmity, we are assayed in the faith and made mighty. For if our faith had no enmity, it should deserve no reward, as to the understanding that I have in all our Lord's meaning.

95

(S) Jesus wills our souls be in glad cheer to him. For his cheer is to us merry and lovely. And how he shows to us three kinds, cheer of passion, compassion, and blissful cheer. The Seventy-First Chapter. (SP)

¶ Glad and merry and sweet is the blissful, lovely cheer of our Lord to our souls. For we must needs ever live in love longing. And he will our soul be in glad cheer to him to give him his reward. ¶ And thus I hope with his grace he has, and more, shall draw the outer cheer to the inner cheer, and make us all at one with him, and each of us with other in true lasting joy, that is Jesus. I have meaning of three kinds of cheer of our Lord. ¶ The first is cheer of Passion, as he showed while he was here in this life dying, though this beholding be mournful and grieving, yet it is glad and merry, for he is God. ¶ The second manner of cheer is pity, ruth, and compassion, and this shows he to all his lovers with secureness of keeping who have need to his mercy. ¶ The third is the blissful cheer as it shall be without end, and this was oftenest and longest continued. ¶ And thus in the time of our pain and our woe he shows us cheer of his Passion and of his Cross, helping us to bear it by his own blessed virtue. And in the time of our sinning, he shows to us cheer of ruth and pity, mightily keeping and defending us against all our enemies. ¶ And these two be the common cheer which he shows to us in this life, therewith meddling the third and that is his blissful cheer like in part as it shall be in heaven. And that is a gracious touching and sweet lighting of the ghostly life, whereby we are kept in sure faith, hope, and charity, with contrition, devotion, and also with contemplation, and all manner of true solace and sweet comforts. ¶ The blissful cheer of our Lord God works it in us by grace.

(S) Sin in the chosen soul is deadly for a time. But they be not dead in the sight of God. And how we have here matter of joy and mourning, and that for our blindness and weight of flesh. And of the most comfortable cheer of God. And why these Showings were made. The Seventy-Second Chapter. (Sp)

But now I need to tell in what manner I saw sin deadly in the creatures who shall not die for sin, but live in the joy of God without end. (SpM) ¶ I saw that two contraries should never be together in one place. The most contrarious are the highest bliss and the deepest pain. ¶ The highest bliss that is, is to have him in clearness of endless life, him truly seeing, sweetly feeling, all perfectly having, in fullness of joy. And thus was the blissful cheer of our Lord showed in pity. In which Showing I saw that sin is most contrary, so much that as long as we be meddled with any part of sin we shall never see clearly the blissful cheer of our Lord. And the more horrible and more grievous 〰️ 96 that our sins be, the deeper are we for that time from this blissful sight. ¶ And therefore it seems to us oftentimes as we were in peril of death in a part of Hell, for the sorrow and pain that the sin is to us. And thus we are dead for the time, from the very sight of our blissful life. But in all this I saw truly that we be not dead in the sight of God nor does he ever pass from us. But he shall never have his full bliss in us, till we have our full bliss in him. ¶ Truly seeing his fair blissful cheer, for we are ordained thereto in nature and get there by grace. ¶ Thus I saw how sin is deadly for a short time in the blessed creatures of endless life. And ever the more clearly that the soul sees this blissful cheer by grace of loving, the more it longs to see it in fullness, that is to say, in his own likeness. ¶ For notwithstanding if our Lord God dwells in us and is here with us and he calls us and encloses us for tender love, that he may never leave us and is more near to us than tongue can tell or heart can think. ¶ Yet may we never cease from mourning nor weeping nor longing till when we see him clearly in his blissful cheer. For in that precious blissful sight there may no woe abide, nor any weal fail. ¶ And in this I saw matter of mirth and matter of mourning. Matter of mirth for our Lord, our Maker, is so near to us, and in us, and we in him by secureness of keeping of his great goodness. ¶ Matter of mourning for our ghostly eye is so blind and we be so borne down by weight of our deadly flesh and darkness of sin that we may not see our Lord God clearly in his fair blissful cheer. ¶ No, and because of this darkness scarce we can believe and trust his great love and our sureness of keeping. ¶ And therefore it is that I say, we may never cease of moaning nor of weeping. This weeping means not all in pouring out of tears by our bodily eye, but also to more ghostly understanding. For the natural desire of our soul is so great and so unmeasurable, that if it were given us to our solace and to our comfort, all the nobility that ever God made in heaven and in earth, and we saw not the fair blissful cheer of himself, yet we should not stint of moaning nor of ghostly weeping, that is to say of painful longing, till when we see truly the fair blissful cheer of our Maker. ¶ And if we were in all the pain that heart can think and tongue may tell, if we might in that time see his fair blissful cheer, all this pain should not grieve us. ¶ Thus is that blissful sight end of all manner of pain to a loving soul and fulfilling all manner of joy and bliss. And that showed he in the high marvelous words where he said, "I it am who is highest, I it am who is lowest, whom you love, I it am who is all." It belongs to us to have three kinds of knowings. ¶ This first

97   is that we know our Lord God. ¶ The second is that we know our self, what we are by him in nature and grace. ¶ The third that we know meekly what our self is regarding our sin and against feebleness. And for these three was all the Showing made as to my understanding.

(S) These Revelations were showed in three ways. And of two ghostly surenesses, of which God will we amend us, remembering his Passion, knowing also he is all love. For he will we have secureness and liking

in love, not taking on unreasonable heaviness for our past sins. (SP)
The Seventy-Third Chapter. (SPH)

All the blessed teaching of our Lord God was showed (H) to me (SPH) by three parts, (H) as I have said before, (SPH) that is to say, by bodily sight, and by word formed in my understanding, and by ghostly sight. For the bodily sight I have said as I saw as truly as I can. ¶ And for the words, I have said them right as our Lord showed them to me. ¶ And for the ghostly sight I have said somewhat, but I may never fully tell it. And therefore of this ghostly sight, I am stirred to say more, as God will give me grace.

¶ {God showed (H) me (SPH) two kinds of sickness that we have, (H) of which he will we be amended. (SPH) ¶ That one is impatience or sloth. For we bear our travail and our pains heavily. ¶ That other is despair or doubtful dread, as I shall say after. ¶ Generally he showed sin wherein that all is comprehended. But in particular he showed not but these two. And these two are they that most travail and tempest us. As by that our Lord showed me. ¶ Of which he will we be amended. I speak of such men and women who, for God's love, hate sin and dispose themselves to do God's will. Then by our ghostly blindness and bodily heaviness we are most inclined to these. (H) Then are these two privy sins and most busy about us. (SPH) ¶ And therefore it is God's will they be known, and then shall we refuse them, as we do other sins. ¶ And for full help of this, full meekly our Lord showed (H) me (SPH) the patience that he had in his hard Passion. And also the joying and the liking that he has of that Passion for love. ¶ And this he showed (H) me (SPH) in example, that we should gladly and wisely bear our pains, for that is greatly pleasing to him and endless profit to us. And the cause why we are travailed with them, is for unknowing of love. Though the three Persons of the Trinity be all equal in the (H) property, Love was most showed to me, that is most near to us all (SP) self, the soul takes most understanding in love. Yea, and he will in all thing that we have our beholding and our enjoying in love. ¶ And of this knowing are we most blind. For (SP) some of us (H) many men and women (SPH) believe that God is Almighty and may do all, and that he is all wisdom and can do all. But that he is all love and will do all, there we stop. ¶ And this unknowing it is that most blocks God's lovers, as to my sight. For when we begin to hate sin and amend us, by the ordinance of holy Church, yet there dwells a dread that stops us from the beholding of ourself, and of our sins done before. ¶ And some of us for our every day sins, for we hold not our covenants nor keep not

98   our cleanness that our Lord sets us in, but fall often in so much wretchedness that it is shame to see it. ¶ And the beholding of this makes us so sorry and so heavy, that scarce we can find any comfort. And this dread we take sometimes for a meekness, but this is a foul blindness and a weakness. And we cannot despise it as we do another sin that we know, for it comes of enmity which comes through lack of true judgment, and it is against truth. For of all the properties of the blissful Trinity it is God's will that we have most secureness and liking in love. ¶ For love makes might and wisdom full meek to us. For right as by the courtesy of God, he forgives our sins following the time that we repent. Right so will he that we forgive our sin as regards our unreasonable heaviness and our doubtful dreads.

(S) There be four kinds of dread, but reverent dread is a lovely truth that never is without meek love. And yet they be not both one. And how we should pray God for the same. (SP) The Seventy-Fourth Chapter. (SPꟙ)

{f}or I understood four manner of dreads. One is the dread of fear that comes to a man suddenly by frailty. This dread does good for it helps to purge man as does bodily sickness, or such other pain that is not sin. For all such pains help man, if they be patiently taken. ¶ The second is dread of pain, whereby man is stirred and wakened from the sleep of sin, he is not able for the time to perceive the soft comfort of the holy Ghost, till he have understanding of this dread of pain of bodily death, and of ghostly enemies, (ꟙ) the fire of Purgatory. (SPꟙ) And this dread stirs us to seek comfort and mercy of God. And thus this dread helps us as an entry, to seek comfort and mercy of God, and enables us to have contrition by the blissful touching of the holy Ghost. ¶ The third is doubtful dread. Doubtful dread inasmuch as it draws to despair. (ꟙ) For though it be little in the self, and it was known it is a spice of despair, for I am sure that all doubtful dreads, God hates. And he will that we have them cast from us with true knowing of life. (SP) God will have it turned in us into love by true knowing of love, that is to say, that the bitterness of doubt be turned into sweetness of natural love by grace. For it may never please our Lord that his servants doubt his goodness. ¶ The fourth is reverent dread, for there is no dread that fully pleases God in us but reverent dread, and that is full (Ⱨ) sweet and (SⱣⱧ) soft. For the more it is had, the less is it felt for sweetness of love. Love and dread are brethren, and they are rooted in us by the goodness of our Maker, and they shall never be taken from us without end. We have of nature to love and we have of grace to love. And we have of nature to dread and we have of grace to dread. It belongs to the Lordship and to the Fatherhood to be dreaded. As it belongs to the goodness to be loved and it belongs to us who are his servants and his children to dread him, for Lordship and Fatherhood as it belongs to us to love him for goodness. (Ⱨ) And though this reverent dread and love (S) be not parted asunder, yet they are (SⱣⱧ) not both one. But they are two in property and in working, and neither of them may be had without the other. Therefore I am sure he who loves, he dreads, though he feels it but a little. All dreads other than reverent dread, that are offered to us, though they come under the colour of holiness, yet are not so true, and hereby may they be known asunder (Ⱨ) and discerned, which is which. For this reverent dread the more it is had, the more it softens and comforts and pleases and rests, and the false dread, it travails and tempests and troubles. (SⱣ) That dread that makes us 🙰🙰🙰 99 hastily to flee from all that is not good, and fall into our Lord's breast as the Child into the Mother's lap with all our intent and with all our mind, knowing our feebleness, and our great need, knowing his everlasting goodness, and his blissful love, only seeking to him for salvation, cleaving to him with secure trust, that dread that brings us into this working, it is natural, gracious, good, and true. And all that is contrarious to this, either it is wrong, or it is meddled with wrong. ¶ Then is this the remedy, to know them both, and refuse the wrong (Ⱨ) false. Right as we would a wicked spirit that showed himself in the likeness of a good angel, for right as an ill spirit though he come under the color and the likeness of a good angel, with his dalliance and his working, though he show never so fair, first he travails and tempests and troubles the person that he speaks with and hinders him and leaves him all in unrest. And the more that he communes with him the more he troubles him, and the farther he is from peace. Therefore it is God's will and our help, that we know them thus asunder. For God will that we be ever secure in love and peaceable and restful, as he is to us. And right so of the same condition as he is to us, so will he that we be to our self. And to our Even-Christian. Amen. Explicit Juliane de Norwyche, Here ends Julian of Norwich. [End Ⱨ] For the natural profit of dread which we have in this life by the gracious working of the holy Ghost, the same shall be in heaven before God, gentle, courteous, and fully delectable. And thus we shall in love be homely and near to God, and we shall in dread be gentle and courteous to God. And both alike even. Desire we of our Lord God to dread him reverently and to love him meekly and to trust in him mightily. For when we dread him reverently and love him meekly our trust is never in vain. ¶ For the more that we trust and the mightier (ꝑ) that we trust, (Sꝑ) the more we please and worship our Lord in whom we trust. And if we fail this reverent dread and meek love (as God forbid we should), our trust shall soon be misruled for the time. And therefore we most need to pray our Lord of grace that we may have this reverent dread and meek love of his gift in heart and in work. For without this no man may please God.

(S) We need love, longing, and pity. And of three kinds of longing in God which are in us. And how at Doomsday the joy of the blessed shall be increased, seeing truly the cause of all things that God has done, dreadfully trembling and thanking him for joy, marveling at the greatness of God, source of all that is made. (Sꝑ) The Seventy-Fifth Chapter.

I saw that God may do all that we need. And these three that I shall say are needed, Love, longing, pity. ¶ Pity in love keeps us in the time of our need. ¶ And longing in the same love draws us into heaven. For the thirst of God is to have the general man into him, in which thirst he has drawn his holy souls who be now in bliss and getting his lively members. Ever he draws and drinks and yet he thirsts and longs. ¶ I saw three kinds of longing in God and all to one end of which we have the same in us and of the same virtue and for the same end. ¶ The first is that he longs to teach us to know him and love him evermore as it is convenient and helpful to us. ¶ The second is that he longs to have us up to his bliss as souls are when they are taken out of pain into heaven. ¶ The third is to fulfill us in bliss, and that shall be fulfilled on the last day to last for ever. 🙰 For I saw as it is known in our faith that the pain and the sorrow shall be ended to all who shall be saved. And not only we shall receive the same bliss the soul had had before in heaven, but also we shall receive a new bliss which plenteously shall be flowing out of God into us, and fulfilling us. And these be the goods which he hath ordained to give us from without beginning. ¶ These goods are

100

treasured and hid in himself. For into that time the creature is not mighty nor worthy enough to receive them. ¶ In this we shall see truly the cause of all things he has done. And ever more we shall see the cause of all things that he has allowed, and the bliss and the fulfilling shall be so deep, and so high, that for wonder and marvel all creatures shall have to God such great reverent dread overpassing what has been seen, and felt before. That the pillars of heaven shall tremble and quake. ¶ But this manner of trembling and dread shall have no pain, but it belongs to the worthy might of God, thus to be beheld of his creatures, dreadfully trembling and quaking for meekness of joy, marveling at the greatness of God the Maker, and of the littleness of all that is made. ¶ For the beholding of this makes the creature marvelously meek and mild. Wherefore God wills, and also it belongs to us both in nature and grace to understand and know of this, desiring this sight and this working, for it leads us in the right way and keeps us in true life and ones us to God. And as good as God is, as great he is. And as much as it belongs to his Godhead to be loved, so much does it belong to his greatness to be dreaded. ¶ For this reverent dread is the fair courtesy that is in heaven before God's face. And as much as he shall then be known and loved overpassing than he is now, in so much he shall be dreaded overpassing than he is now. ¶ Wherefore it needs must be that all heaven, all earth, shall tremble and quake when the pillars shall tremble and quake.

(S) A loving soul hates sin for vileness more than all the pains of Hell. And how the beholding of another man's sin (but if it be with compassion) stops the beholding of God. And the devil by putting in remembrance our wretchedness would stop it in the same way. And of our sloth. (SP) The Seventy-Sixth Chapter.

I speak but little of reverent dread, for I hope it may be seen in this matter beforesaid. ¶ But well I know our Lord showed me no souls but those who dread him. For well I know the soul who truly takes the teaching of the holy Ghost, it hates sin more for vileness and horribleness, than it does all the pain that is in Hell. ¶ For the soul who beholds the nature of our Lord Jesus, it hates no Hell but sin, as to my sight. ¶ And therefore it is God's will that we know sin, and pray busily and travail wilfully, and seek teaching meekly, that we fall not blindly

101 therein. ¶ And if we fall that we rise readily. For it is the most pain that the soul may have to turn from God any time by sin. ¶ The soul who will be in rest, when other man's sin comes to my mind, he shall flee from it as the pain of Hell, seeking into God for remedy for help against it. For the beholding of other men's sins, it makes as it were a thick mist before the eye of the soul, and we may not for the time see the fairness of God. But, if we may behold him, with contrition with him, with compassion on him, and with holy desire to God for him. For without this it annoys and tempests and blocks the soul that beholds them. For this is understood in the Showing of compassion. In this blissful Showing of our Lord, I have understanding of two contraries. ¶ That one is the most wisdom that any creature may do in this life, that other is the most folly. The most wisdom is for a creature to do after the will and counsel of his highest sovereign friend. ¶ This blessed friend is Jesus, and it is his will and his counsel that we hold us with him, and fasten us homely to him, evermore, in whatsoever state we be. For whether we be foul or clean, we are all one in his loving. For weal nor for woe he will that never we flee from him. But for the changeability that we are in our self we fall often into sin. Then we have this by the stirring of the enemy, and by our own folly and blindness. For they say thus, "You know well you are a wretch, a sinner, and also untrue, for you keep not the command. You promised our Lord often that you shall do better and immediately after you fall again in the same, namely in sloth, in losing of time." For that is the beginning of sin, as to my sight. And namely to the creatures who have given themselves to serve our Lord with inward beholding of his blessed goodness. ¶ And this makes us dread to appear before our courteous Lord. Then it is our enemy who will put us back with his false dread of our wretchedness, for pain that he threatens us by. ¶ For it is his meaning to make us so heavy and so weary in this that we should blot out of mind the fair blissful beholding of our everlasting friend.

***

(S) Of the enmity of the fiend who loses more in our uprising than he wins by our falling and therefore he is scorned. And how the scourge of God should be suffered with mind of his Passion. For that is especially rewarded above penance chosen by our self. And we must needs have woe, but courteous God is our leader, keeper, and bliss. (ᛋᛈ) The Seventy-Seventh Chapter.

Our good Lord showed the enmity of the fiend whereby I understood that all that is contrarious to love and to peace it is the fiend and of his party. And we have of our feebleness and our folly to fall, and we have of mercy and grace of the holy Ghost to rise to more joy. ¶ And if our enemy wins out over us by our falling, for this is his liking, he loses ⚏ manifold more in our rising by charity and meekness. And this glorious rising is to him so great sorrow and pain for the hate he has to our soul that he burns continually in envy. And all this sorrow that he would make us have, it shall turn upon himself. And for this it was that our Lord scorned him. And this made me mightily to laugh. Then is this the remedy, that we be to know our wretchedness and flee to our Lord. For ever the more needy that we be, the more helpful it is to us to draw near him. And say we thus in our meaning, "I know well I have a shrewd pain, but our Lord is Almighty and may punish me mightily. And he is all Wisdom and can punish me skillfully. And he is all Goodness and loves me tenderly. And in this beholding it is necessary for us to abide. For it is a lovely meekness of a sinful soul wrought by mercy and grace of the holy Ghost when we will wilfully and gladly take the scourge and chastening of our Lord. He himself will give it to us, and it shall be full tender and full easy, if that we will only hold us paid with him and with all his works. ¶ For the penance that man takes of himself was not showed me, that is to say, it was not showed me specified. ¶ But it was showed specially and highly and with full lovely cheer, that we shall meekly and patiently bear and suffer the penance that God himself gives us with mind in his blessed Passion. ¶ For when we have mind in his blessed Passion with pity and love, then we suffer with him as his friends did who saw it. ¶ And this was showed in the Thirteenth Showing near at the beginning, where it speaks of pity. For he says, "Accuse not yourself over much, demanding that tribulation and your woe is all for your fault. For I will not that you be heavy nor sorrowful indiscreetly. For I tell you how so you do you shall have woe. ¶ And therefore I will that you wisely know your penance, and shall then truly see that all your living is profitable penance." This place is prison and this life is penance, and in the remedy he will we enjoy. ¶ The remedy is that our Lord is with us keeping and leading us into the fullness of joy. For this is an endless joy to us in our Lord's meaning, that he who shall be our bliss when we are there, he is our keeper while we are here. Our way and our heaven is true love and secure trust.

102

¶ And of this he gave understanding in all and namely in the Showing of his Passion, where he made me mightily to choose him for my heaven. ¶ Flee we to our Lord and we shall be comforted, touch we him and we shall be made clean, cleave to him and we shall be sure and safe from all manner of peril. ¶ For our courteous Lord wills that we be as homely with him as heart may think or soul may desire. ¶ But beware that we take not so recklessly this homeliness, that we leave courtesy. For our Lord himself is sovereign homeliness and as homely as he is as courteous he is, for he is very courtesy. ¶ And the blessed creatures that shall be in heaven with him without end, he will have them like to himself in all things. And to be like our Lord perfectly, it is our very salvation and our full bliss. And if we know not how we shall do all this, desire we of our Lord and he shall teach us. For it is his own liking and his worship, blessed must he be.

103

(S) Our Lord will we know four kinds of goodness that he does to us and how we need the light of grace to know our sin and feebleness for we are nothing of our self but wretchedness, and we may not know the horribleness of sin as it is. And how our enemy would we should never know our sin till the last day, wherefore we are much bound to God who shows it now. (SP) The Seventy-Eighth Chapter.

Our Lord of his mercy shows us our sin and our feebleness by the sweet gracious light of himself. For our sin is so vile and so horrible that he of his courtesy will not show it to us but by the light of his grace and mercy. ¶ Of four things it is his will that we have knowing. ¶ The first is that he is our ground of whom we have all our life and our being. ¶ The second that he keeps us mightily and mercifully in the time that we are in our sin and among all our enemies who are full fierce upon us. And so much we are in the more peril, for we give them occasion thereto and know not our own need. ¶ The third is how courteously he keeps us and makes us to know that we have gone amiss. ¶ The fourth is how steadfastly he abides us and changes no cheer. For he will that we be turned and oned to him in love as he is to us. ¶ And thus by this gracious knowing we may see our sin profitably without despair, for truly we need to see it, and by the sight we shall be made

ashamed of ourself and broken down as regards our pride and presumption. For we need truly to see that of our self we are right nought
but sin, and wretchedness. And thus by the sight of the less that our
Lord shows us the more is wasted which we see not. For he of his courtesy measures the sight to us. ¶ For it is so vile and so horrible that we
should not endure to see it as it is. ¶ And thus by this meek knowing
through contrition and grace we shall be broken from all things that are
not our Lord. ¶ And then shall our blessed Saviour perfectly heal us
and one us to him. ¶ This breaking and this healing our Lord means by
the general man. ¶ For he who is highest and nearest with God, he may
see himself sinful, and needful with me. ¶ And I that am the least and
lowest of those who shall be saved, I may be comforted with him who
is highest. So has our Lord oned us in charity. ¶ When he showed me
that I should sin, and for joy that I had in beholding of him, I heeded
not readily to that Showing, and our courteous Lord stopped there and
would not teach me further, till he gave me grace and will to attend. ¶
And hereof was I taught, though that we be highly lifted up into contemplation by the special gift of our Lord, yet we need therewith to
have knowing, and sight of our sin and our feebleness. For without this
knowing we may not have true meekness and without this we may not
be saved. ¶ And also I saw that we may not have this knowing of our
self, nor of none of all our ghostly enemies, for they will us not so much
good. ¶ For if it were by their will we should not see it until our
dying day. ¶ Then we be much bound to God that he will himself for
love show it to us in time of mercy and grace.

104

(S) We are taught to know our sin and not to our neighbours but for
their help. And God will we know what ever stirring we have contrary
to this Showing it comes of our enemy. For the great love of God knows
we should not be the more reckless to fall and if we fall we must hastily
rise or else we are greatly unnatural to God. (SP) The Seventy-Ninth
Chapter.

Also I had in this more understanding in that he showed me that I
should sin. I took it nakedly to my own singular person. For I was
none otherwise stirred at the time. But by the high gracious comfort of

our Lord that followed after, I saw that his meaning was for the general man, that is to say to all man who is sinful and shall be into the last day, of which man I am a member, as I hope, by the mercy of God. For the blessed comfort that I saw it is large enough for us all. ¶ And here was I taught that I should see my own sin and not other men's sins, but if it may be for comfort and help of my even-Christian. ¶ And also in this same Showing where I saw that I should sin, then was I taught to be full of dread for unsecureness of my self. For I know not how I shall fall, nor I know not the measure nor the greatness of sin. For that would I have understood fearfully. And thereto I had no answer. ¶ Also our courteous Lord in the same time, he showed full securely and mightily the endlessness and the unchangeability of his love. ¶ And also by his great goodness and his grace inwardly keeping that the love of him and our soul shall never be departed in two without end. And thus in this dread I have matter of meekness that saves me from presumption. And in the blessed Showing of Love I have matter of true comfort and of joy, that saves me from despair. ¶ All this homely showing of our courteous Lord, it is a lovely lesson and a sweet gracious teaching of himself in comforting of our soul. ¶ For he will that we know by the sweetness and homely loving of him, that all that we see or feel within or without which is contrarious to this is of the enemy, and not of God. As thus. ¶ If we be stirred to be the more reckless of our living, or of the keeping of our hearts by the cause that we have knowing of this plenteous love, then we need greatly to beware. For this stirring, if it come, it is untrue, and greatly we ought to hate it, for it all has no likeness of God's will. ¶ And when we fall by frailty or blindness, then our courteous Lord touches us, stirs us, and calls us, and then will that we see our wretchedness, and meekly be it known. But he wills not we abide thus, nor wills he that we busy us greatly about our accusing, nor he will that we be wretched of our self. But he wills that we hastily heed him. ⬛ For he stands all alone, and waits for us, mourning and moaning, till when we come, and has haste to have us to him. For we are his joy and his delight and he is our salve and our life. ¶ Though I say he stands all alone, I leave the speaking of the blessed company of heaven, and speak of his office and his working here on earth, upon the condition of the Showing.

105

(S) By three things God is worshiped and we saved, and how our know-ing now is but as an ABC. And sweet Jesus does all, abiding and moan-ing with us. But when we are in sin Christ moans alone. Then it belongs to us for kindness and reverence hastily to turn to him again. (Sp) The Eightieth Chapter.

By three things man stands in this life, by which three God is wor-shiped and we be helped, kept, and saved. ¶ The first is use of man's natural reason. ¶ The second is common teaching of the holy Church. ¶ The third is inward gracious working of the holy Ghost. And these three be all of one God. ¶ God is the ground of our natural reason, and God the teaching of holy Church; and God is the holy Ghost. And all be sundry gifts to which he will we have great regard and heed us thereto. ¶ For these work in us continually all together and these be great things. Of which great things he will we have knowing here as it were in one ABC, that is to say that we have a little knowing whereof we shall have fullness in heaven. And that is for to help us. ¶ We know in our faith that God alone took our nature and none but he. And furthermore that Christ alone did all the works that belong to our sal-vation and none but he. And right so he alone does now the last end, that is to say he dwells here with us, and rules us and governs us in this life and brings us to his bliss. And thus shall he do as long as any soul is in earth who shall come to heaven. ¶ And so much so that if there were no such soul with him but one he should be all alone till he had bought him up to his bliss. ¶ I believe and understand the ministra-tions of angels as clergy tell, but it was not showed to me. For himself is nearest, and meekest, highest and lowest, and does all. And not only all that we need but also he does all that is worshipful to our joy in heaven. And where I say he waits mourning and moaning, it means all the true feeling that we have in our self in contrition and compassion, and all mourning and moaning that we are not oned with our Lord. And all such that is helpful it is Christ in us. And though some of us feel it seldom, it passes never from Christ, till what time he has brought us out of all our woe. For love suffers never to be without pity. ¶ And what time that we fall into sin and leave the mind of him and the keep-ing of our own soul, then Christ alone keeps all the charge of us, and thus he stands mourning and moaning. ¶ Then it belongs to us for rev-erence and nature to turn us hastily to our Lord and leave him not alone. He is here 𝔖𝔍𝔈 alone with us all. That is to say, only for us he is here. ¶ And what time I am withdrawn from him by sin, despair, or sloth, then I let my Lord stand alone inasmuch as it is in me. ¶ And thus it fares

106

with us all, who be sinners. But though it be so that we do thus often, his goodness suffers us never to be alone, but lastingly he is with us, and tenderly he excuses us, and ever shields us from blame in his sight.

(S) This blessed woman saw God in diverse manners. But she saw him take no resting place but in man's soul. And he will we enjoy more in his love than sorrow for often falling, remembering reward everlasting and living gladly in penance. And why God allows sin. (SP) The Eighty-First Chapter.

Our good Lord showed him in divers ways, both in heaven, in earth, but I saw him take no place but in man's soul. He showed him in earth, in the sweet Incarnation and in his blessed Passion. And in other ways he showed him in earth where I said "I saw God in a point." And in other ways he showed him on earth, thus, as it were in a pilgrimage, that is to say he is here with us, leading us, and shall be till when he has brought us all to his bliss in heaven. ¶ He showed him divers times reigning, as it is said before. But principally in man's soul, he has taken there his resting place and his worshipful city. ¶ Out of which worshipful see he shall never rise nor remove without end. Marvelous and solemn is the place where the Lord dwells, and therefore he will that we readily heed to his gracious touching, more enjoying in his whole love, than sorrowing for our frequent fallings. For it is the most worship to him of any thing that we may do that we believe gladly and merrily for his love in our penance. For he beholds us so tenderly that he sees all our living and penance. For natural loving is to him always lasting penance in us, which penance he works in us, and mercifully he helps us to bear it. ¶ For his love makes him to long, his wisdom and his truth with his righteousness makes him to suffer us here, and in this way he will see it in us. For this is our natural penance and the highest as to my sight. ¶ For this penance comes never from us till what time we be fulfilled, when we shall have him to our reward. ¶ And therefore he wills that we set our hearts in the overpassing, that is to say, from the pain that we feel into the bliss that we trust.

(S) God beholds the moaning of the soul with pity and not with blame. And yet we do nought but sin in which we are kept ▨▨▨ in solace and in dread. For he will we turn to him, readily cleaving to his love, seeing that he is our medicine. And so we must love in longing and in enjoying. And whatsoever is contrary to this is not of God but of enmity. (SP) The Eighty-Second Chapter.

107

But here showed our courteous Lord the moaning and the mourning of the soul meaning thus, "I know well you will live for my love, merrily and gladly suffering all the penance that may come to you. But inasmuch as you live not without sin, you would suffer for my love all the woe, all the tribulation and disease that might come to you and it is true. But be not greatly grieved with sin that comes about against your will." ¶ And here I understood that, that the Lord beholds the servant with pity and not with blame. For this passing life asks not to live all without blame and sin. ¶ He loves us endlessly and we sin habitually and he shows us full mildly. And then we sorrow and mourn, discreetly turning ourselves into the beholding of his mercy, cleaving to his love and goodness, seeing that he is our medicine, knowing that we do nought but sin. ¶ And thus by the meekness that we get by the sight of our sin faithfully, knowing his everlasting love, him thanking and praising, we please him. ¶ "I love you, and you love me, and our love shall not be parted in two. And for your profit I suffer." And all this was showed in ghostly understanding, saying these blessed words, "I keep you full securely." And by great desire that I have in our blessed Lord that we shall live in this manner, that is to say, in longing and enjoying. As all this lesson of love shows thereby, I understood that all that is contrarious to us, is not of him, but of enmity. And he will that we know it by the sweet gracious light of his natural love. ¶ If any such lover be in earth, who is continually kept from falling I know it not. For it was not showed me. ¶ But this was showed, that in falling and in rising we are ever preciously kept in one love. ¶ For in the beholding of God we fall not, and in the beholding of our self we stand not. And both these be true, as to my sight. But the beholding of our Lord God is the highest truth. Then are we much bound to God, that he will in this living show us this high truth. And I understood that while we be in this life it is most helpful to us that we see both these at once. ¶ For the higher beholding keeps us in ghostly solace and true enjoying in God. ¶ That other that is the lower beholding keeps us in dread and makes us ashamed of our self. But our good Lord will ever that we hold us much more in the beholding ▨▨▨ of the higher, and not believe the

108

knowing of the lower. Into the time that we be brought up above where we shall have our Lord Jesus unto our reward and be fulfilled of joy and bliss without end.

(S) Of three properties in God, Life, Love, and Light. And that our reason is in God according it its highest gift, and how our faith is a light coming of the Father, measured to us and in this night leading us. And the end of our woe. Suddenly our eye shall be opened in full light and clearness of sight who is our Maker, Father and holy Ghost in Jesus our Saviour. (Sp) The Eighty-Third Chapter.

I had in part touching, sight, and feeling in three properties of God, in which the strength and effect of all the Revelation stands. And they were seen in every Showing, and most properly in the Twelfth where it says often, "I it am." The properties are these, "life, love, and light." In life is marvelous homeliness, and in love is gentle courtesy, and in light is endless kindness. These three properties were in one goodness, into which goodness my reason would be oned and cleave to with all its might. ¶ I beheld with reverent dread, and highly marveling in the sight and in the feeling of the sweet accord that our reason is in God, understanding that it is the highest gift that we have received. And it is grounded in nature. ¶ Our faith is a light naturally coming of our endless day, that is our Father God, in which light our Mother Christ, and our good Lord, the holy Ghost, lead us in this passing life. ¶ The light is measured discreetly, needfully standing to us in the night. The light is cause of our life, the night is cause of our pain and of all our woe, in which we deserve reward and thank of God. For we with mercy and grace, wilfully know and believe our light going therein wisely and mightily. And at the end of woe suddenly our eye shall be opened, and in clearness of light our sight shall be full. Which light is God our Maker, and holy Ghost in Christ Jesus our Saviour. ¶ Thus I saw and understood that our faith is our light in our night, which light is God our endless day.

(S) Charity is this light which is not so little but that it is needful with travail to deserve endless worshipful thanks of God. For faith and hope lead us to charity which is in two kinds. (Sp) The Eighty-Fourth Chapter.

This light is charity, and the measuring of this light is done to us profitably by the wisdom of God. For neither the light is so large that we may see our blissful day, nor is it kept from us, but it is such a light in which we may live rewarded with travail deserving the endless worship of God. And this was seen in the Sixth Showing where he said, "I thank you for your service and of your travail." Thus charity keeps us in faith and in hope, and faith and hope leads us in charity. And at the end all shall be charity. ¶ I had three manner of understanding charity in this light. ¶ The first is charity unmade. ¶ The second is charity made. ¶ The third is charity given. Charity unmade is God. Charity made is our soul in God. Charity given is virtue. And that is a gracious gift of working in which we love God, for himself, and our selves in God, and all that God loves for God.

(S) God loved his chosen from without beginning. And he never suffers them to be hurt, whereof their bliss might be lessened. And how privities now hid in heaven shall be known. Wherefore we shall bless our Lord that every thing is so well ordained. (Sp) The Eighty-Fifth Chapter.

And in this sight I marveled highly. For notwithstanding our simple living and our blindness here, yet endlessly our courteous Lord beholds us in this working, enjoying. ¶ And of all things we may please him best, wisely, and truly, to believe it and to enjoy with him, and in him. ¶ For as truly as we shall be in the bliss of God without end, him praising and thanking, as truly we have been in the foresight of God loved and known in his endless purpose, from without beginning, in which unbegun love he made us, and in the same love he keeps us, and never suffers us to be hurt, by which our bliss might be lessened. ¶ And therefore when the Doom is given, and we be all brought up above, then we clearly see in God the privities which be now hid to us. Then shall none of us be stirred to say in any way, "Lord, if it had been thus, then it had been full well." ¶ But we shall all say without voice, "Lord,

109

blessed must you be. ¶ For it is thus. It is well. And now we see truly that all thing is done as it was then ordained before that any thing was made."

(S) The good Lord showed this book should be otherwise performed than at the first writing. And for his working he will we thus pray, him thanking, trusting, and in him enjoying. And how he made this Showing because he will have it known. In which knowing he will give us grace to love him. For fifteen years after it was answered that the cause of all this Showing was love, which Jesus must grant us. Amen. (SP) The Eighty-Sixth Chapter.

This book is begun by God's gift and his grace, but it is not yet performed as to my sight. For charity pray we all together with God's working, thanking, trusting, enjoying. For thus will our good Lord be prayed. As by the understanding that I took in all his own meaning and in the sweet words where he says full merrily, "I am ground of your prayer." For truly I saw and understood in our Lord's meaning, that he showed it, for he will have it known more than it is. ¶ In which knowing he will give us grace to love him and cleave to him. For he beholds his heavenly treasure with so great love on earth, that he will give us more light and solace in heavenly joy, in drawing of our hearts for sorrow and darkness which we are in. ¶ And from that time that it was showed I desired oftentimes to know what was our Lord's meaning. ¶ And fifteen years after and more I was answered in ghostly understanding, saying thus, "Would you know 🪷 your Lord's meaning in this thing? Know it well, love was his meaning. Who showed it to you? Love. What did he show you? Love. Why did he show it to you? For Love. Hold yourself therein, and you shall understand and know more of the same. But you shall never know or understand therein other things without end." Thus was I taught that Love was our Lord's meaning. And I saw full surely in this, and in all, that before God made us he loved us, which love was never slaked nor never shall be. ¶ And in this love he has done all his work, and in this love he has made all things profitable to us. And in this love our life is everlasting. ¶ In our making we had beginning. But the love wherein he made us, was in him from without beginnings. ¶ In which love we have our beginning.

110

And all this shall be seen in God without end. Which Jesus must grant us. Amen.

(Ꝑ) Deo gracias. **Thanks be to God.** Explicit liber revelacionum Julyane anatorite norwyche cuius anime propicietur deus. Here ends the Book of Showings of Julian, Anchoress of Norwich, upon whose soul may God have mercy.

(S) Thus ends the Revelation of Love of the blessed Trinity showed by our Saviour Christ Jesus for our endless comfort and solace and also to enjoy in him in this passing journey of this life. Amen. Jesus. Amen.

I pray Almighty God that this book come not but to the hands of them who will be his faithful lovers, and to those who will submit them to the faith of holy Church, and obey the wholesome understanding and teaching of the men who be of virtuous life, serious age, and profound learning. For this Revelation is High Divinity, and high wisdom; wherefore it may not dwell with him who is thrall to sin and to the devil. And beware you take not one thing after your affection and liking and leave another, for that is the condition of a heretic. But take every thing with other, and truly understand. All is according to holy Scripture and grounded in the same, and that Jesus, our very love, light and truth, shall show to all clean souls who with meekness ask perseveringly this wisdom of him. And you to whom this book shall come thank highly and heartily our Saviour Christ Jesus that he made these Showings and Revelations for you and to you of his endless love, mercy and goodness, for your and our safe guide and conduct to everlasting bliss, the which Jesus must grant us. Amen.

Index